The Osu Caste
Discrimination in Igboland

The Osu Caste Discrimination in Igboland

◆

Impact on Igbo Culture and Civilization

Victor E. Dike

iUniverse, Inc.
New York Lincoln Shanghai

The Osu Caste Discrimination in Igboland
Impact on Igbo Culture and Civilization

iUniverse books may be ordered through booksellers or by contacting:

iUniverse
2021 Pine Lake Road, Suite 100
Lincoln, NE 68512
www.iuniverse.com
1-800-Authors (1-800-288-4677)

Because of the dynamic nature of the Internet, any Web addresses or links contained in this book may have changed since publication and may no longer be valid.

The views expressed in this work are solely those of the author and do not necessarily reflect the views of the publisher, and the publisher hereby disclaims any responsibility for them.

ISBN: 978-0-595-45921-6 (pbk)
ISBN: 978-0-595-90221-7 (ebk)

Printed in the United States of America

To the Victims of Discrimination

We are discussing no small matter, but how we ought to live and why. Socrates (as reported by Plato) in the *Republic* (Ca. 390 B.C)

Contents

Preface

"There is no cause half so sacred as the cause of a people. There is no idea so uplifting as the idea of the service of humanity" Winston Churchill.

The Osu Caste Discrimination in Igboland: Impact on Igbo Culture and *Civilization* is a unique publication that deals with the ancient, obnoxious and discriminatory Osu caste system in Igboland. The explosive positive response to the author's first book on this subject in 2002 was encouraging. Using a combination of insights from readers and new theories, this book is designed to offer fuller and deeper understanding of the system and to offer a solution to the naughty issue.

Most of us go through life everyday without being conscious of the innumerable ways in which we are privileged by our birth or ancestry. However, those born into the Osu caste family are not that lucky because in some villages the so-called Osu cannot pass a day without being reminded of his or her status. Thus, as Philo notes, "Be kind, for everyone you meet is fighting a hard battle."

One of the primary objectives of this book is to educate the world about the primitive and obnoxious Osu caste system and to find a lasting solution to the vexing issue. It urges the Igbos' to fight the Osu injustice and discrimination and change Igbo society for the better. Of what use is the discriminatory system? Does any person like to be discriminated against? These are some of the questions this book attempts to address.

There is a false impression in some quarters that the Osu caste system has been abolished in Igboland. For instance, an official of the Nigerian Human Rights Commission, whom this author met in Geneva, in August 2002, at the United Nation Conference on the Elimination of Racial Discrimination, argued that the system has been abolished. This author, who was at the conference to present a paper on the Osu caste system in Igboland, confronted the official with relevant documentation to prove that the system remains.

This book also deals with the ethical aspect of the Osu caste discrimination. Ethics (the study of an ideal human conduct) is a fundamental part of the life of a community, institutions and professional roles. Philosophers and Theologians who study ethics (ethicists) go the extra mile in understanding morality and its implication in every day life. We will become ethicists as we apply some ethical tools in analyzing the effect of the Osu caste system on the lives of the victims and the Igbo society in general.

This book is expected to be valuable to teachers and students in the department of social sciences in higher institutions, to policymakers and researchers and the general reader for a better understanding of the issue and the rich Igbo culture. The questions in the *Making Connections* section are designed for this particular purpose. This book does not pretend to provide all solution to the Osu caste discrimination-it is a minute contribution to the complex and vexing issue.

Acknowledgment

Over the years, I have learned from individuals and influenced by the work of many scholars. Many people offered some useful suggestions, critiqued the work, and assisted in many other ways to enhance the readability of this book. I am particularly grateful to Prof. Enwere Dike, Department of Economics, Nnamdi Azikiwe University, Awka for his encouragement and advice and to Chief Martins Nnadiegbulam Nwoke for reviewing the final draft of the manuscript. Many thanks are also due to Dr. Johnny A. Mez, Chief Nkemdirim C. Ugbaja, Chief (Sir), Dr. and Lady, Lolo Inno Ekeh, Chief Adolf Obilor, and Prof. Peter Nkeonye, Department of Chemistry, Ahmadu Bello Univ., Zaria, Nigeria for their support.

To the authors of the many excellent books on discrimination upon which I launch this quest for justice for the oppressed, I say thank you! This book belongs to the lovers of justice and the entire Dike family because without their support this project would not have been possible. If all these persons who assisted in one way or another to make this project a reality, could not make this book perfect, the fault and errors are solely mine.

Victor E. Dike
Elk Grove, California
May 7, 2007

1

Introduction: The Osu Caste Discrimination in Igboland

I wrote with tears and anguish, pouring into the pages all the pain that life had meant to me (UPTON SINCLAIR).

This chapter deals with general description of the Osu caste system in Igboland and the background for the discourse. As human beings we all have desires, aspirations and purpose; and a genuine purpose always starts with an impulse.[1] And an impulse could be triggered by personal experience or the sufferings of other people and challenges posed by their conditions.

Location of the Igbo Nation

Since the discourse centers on Igbo society it is deemed appropriate to begin the discussion by identifying the location of the Igboland. The Igbo' nation (Igbo society) or (Alaigbo/Anaigbo) is mostly located in the Southeastern and South-central part of Nigeria.

The Igalas and Tivs border the Igboland in the North, the Ijaws in the Southeast, the Efiks and the Ibibios in the East, and the Binis in the West.[2] Most of the Igbos' are Christians, but some of them practice the Igbo traditional religion. The Igbo traditional religion is indigenous—a tribal religion—whose major tenets are shared by all Igbo-speaking people of Nigeria. And the traditional Igbo religion is passed on to succeeding generations. The advent of Christianity in Igboland around 1885 had little or no influence on their traditional beliefs.

The Igbos, generally, are people of the same race and speak the same language. However, the Osu caste system, which is gushing with prejudice and discrimination, has divided and alienated the people. By the late 20th century the population of the Igbos is estimated to about 27 million.[3] Prejudice leads to hatred and

1

often to actions that could harm those that are hated. Such actions are called discrimination[4] and so is the problem with victims of the Osu caste system.

Methodology

Every academic research adopts a methodology or a combination of methodologies on which to base its work from the available research methods and this study is not an exception. Therefore, the qualitative (descriptive) research method is adopted for this work. A descriptive, narrative, and evaluative method allows this author the flexibility to conduct an in-depth analysis, from multiple sources, on the complex and vexing Osu caste problem in Igboland. According to Lofland, et. al, qualitative research method "involves data collection and analysis that are non-quantitative"[5]. Sources of data for qualitative exploration include government documents, newspaper and journal articles, case studies, personal experience, and formal and informal interviews.

This author is, however, aware of the limitations of qualitative method, which centers on validity question, because experts have noted that it is often difficult to determine the truthfulness of qualitative research findings. In spite of this limitation, the qualitative method is still useful. Ronald J. Chenail[6] notes that "the beauty of qualitative inquiry is that by asking simple questions" one gets "complex answers" to resolve complex problems.

The Osu Caste Discrimination in Igboland: Impact on Igbo Culture and Civilization is a fusion of information and ideas from multiple sources. As noted earlier, the author utilized primary and secondary sources to recapture and discuss the historical facts of the Osu caste system and its attendant stigmatization and discrimination in Igboland. These sources were critically reviewed and studied to ensure their validity; and because of the nature of the study this method appears convenient and effective.

Definition of Terms

It is essential to begin this discourse by defining and clarifying the main and associated terms with the system. Without this it would be difficult for readers unfamiliar with the system to understand the concept. Ethnic nationalities within and without Nigeria have varied reasons for discriminating against their own people. Some of them are based on religious belief, culture, and language, among others. The Igbos' discriminate against each other by primary reason of the Osu caste system.

Different parts of Igboland refer to the Osu in varied names: it is Adu-Ebo in Nzam in Onitsha (this is the mixture of Igbo and Igala language) and in the Nsukka area it is Oruma (slaves for the gods). At Awgwu area it is called Nwani or Ohualusi and it is referred to as Osu, Ume, Ohu at Orlu and Owerri areas. It does not matter whether it is referred to as Osu, Ume, Ohu, Oru, Ohu Ume and Omoni (Okpu-Aja) as used or applied in different parts of Igboland these names connote lower and unclean class, or sub-human being.[7]

Some of the terms associated with the Osu system include:

Osu: It has varied definitions; it is a 'cult slave;' a 'child,' 'slave' or 'property' of a god or a deity [8] and living sacrifice'—'a sacrificial lamb.'[9,10,11] An Osu is an out-cast, untouchable, owner's cult, a slave of the deity, and a sacred and holy being. In No Longer at Ease, Okonkwu made his erudite son, Obi, to understand that the "Osu is like leprosy in the minds of our people." An Osu is similar to the Indian untouchables. Oddly, it is an abomination in Igboland for the Diala to marry the Osu because they are deemed unclean. And at a lecture in Nekede (a town near Owerri, Imo State) Jude Ezeala made the world to understand that the "Osu" "are psychologically abused...."[12]

The term "Osu" is better explained than defined, and that shall be done in the next section. Diala: The Diala is a freeborn (non-osu) in Igboland, while the Osu is the "Slave" to the gods. Chukwu, Obasi, Chi, Chineke: Creator God or the "Supreme God" Chinua Achebe.[13] The Igbos' believe in the 'earth goddess,' deities and spirits and also believe in the Chukwu, Obasi, Chi and Chineke or the "Supreme God." Caste: It is "a social category in which membership is fixed at birth and usually unchangeable." A social status or position conferred by a system based on class; status stratified according to ritual purity a social class separated from others by distinctions of hereditary rank or profession or wealth. Caste is derived from the Portuguese word *casta*—meaning lineage, breed or race.[14, 15]

Civil Rights: 'Civil rights are rights that are bestowed by nations on those within their territorial boundaries.' A civil rights is an enforceable right or privilege. And, civil rights sometimes mean nonpolitical rights granted by law, such as basic economic and social rights. The "state has a role in ensuring that all citizens of a society have equal protection under the law and equal opportunity to exercise the privileges of citizenship regardless of race, religion, sex, or other characteristics unrelated to the worth of the individual."[16] These, among others, are freedom of speech, press, assembly, the right to vote, and the freedom of association with others.

Civil rights are considered the cornerstone of a free society; it indicates ways in which a society protects an individual's freedom.[17]

The rights that go with citizenship that one enjoys are not always inalienable rights, because a citizen may lose the right to vote if convicted of certain crimes. Civil rights include all rights that human beings have received from nature that the government or another human being cannot arbitrarily take away, unless deprived by a guilty sentence or death.

Culture: For centuries culture has been variedly defined as the norms, values, customs practices and beliefs of people living within a community. Culture is "the totality of socially transmitted behavior patterns, arts, beliefs, institutions, and all other products of human work and thought."[18] It is also "the set of definitions of reality held in common by people who share a distinctive way of life."[19] However, Apolo Nsibambi defines culture as the customs, mores, values, life styles and practices of a society.[20]

Discrimination: This is "Unfair treatment of a person or group on the basis of prejudice."[21] It is also "Treating people in a different, usually bad, manner because of their class, race, gender or some other category instead of who they are as individuals."[22] As the United Nations notes "Discrimination includes any conduct based on a distinction made on grounds of natural or social categories that have no relation either to individual capacities or merits, or to the concrete behavior of the individual person."[23,24]

Discriminatory practices include inequality in freedom of movement and choice of residence, inequality in the right of peaceful association, inequality in the enjoyment of the right to marry and establish a family, (and) inequality in access to public office ... slavery.[25]

Prejudice: The term, prejudice, is derived from a Latin noun, *praejudicium*, which means precedent.[26] Prejudice is the process of "pre-judging" something. It implies judgment on a subject before learning where the preponderance of the evidence actually lies, or formation of a judgment without direct or actual experience. Thus, prejudice is a judgment formed before due examination and consideration of the facts; it is a premature or hasty judgment about something. Prejudice is:

> An aversive or hostile attitude toward a person who belongs to a group, simply because he belongs to that group, and is therefore presumed to have the objectionable qualities ascribed to the group.[27]

Two essential ingredients associated with prejudice are belief and attitude. A negatively held belief leads to negatively held attitude and that attitude may lead to discrimination, which is the unfair and unequal treatment of people, because of their so-called "bad" traits. It is a differential treatment of individuals or groups not based on actual merit.

Bias: This is "a partiality that prevents objective consideration of an issue or situation."[28] It is "a highly personal and unreasoned distortion of judgmen."[29]

Civilization: By definition, civilization is simply any human society that has produced a state—a political and social body that supersedes the loyalties and functions of the food-gathering clan, of herding tribes, and of the food-producing village. Thus, civilization is a society that has made advances in arts, science and technology, law or government.[30] It is also "a stage of cultural development ..." and "cultural characteristic of a particular time or place" and "refinement of thought, manners, or taste."[31]

Human Rights: These are the basic entitlement accorded to every human being. They include the right to life, the right to health, the rights to education, shelter, employment, property, food, and freedom of expression, association and movement. Others are the rights to an adequate standard of living, freedom from torture and other mistreatment, freedom of religion and assembly, the right to self-determination, and the right of participation in cultural and political life.[32]

Article 1 of the Universal Declaration of Human Rights introduces the words "dignity, justice and equality." Human rights are legal, political, and moral claims to conditions necessary for the well being of a people. And philosophically, human rights are based on the concepts of human dignity and non-discrimination among individuals. Legally, these rights are based on national constitutions, laws and treaties that oblige governments and individuals to behave in certain ways.[33]

As Eleanor Roosevelt notes, "Human rights are a fundamental object of law and government in a just society."[34] Claude Ake[35] noted that human beings have certain rights simply by virtue of being human beings. For that, individuals are entitled to, and indeed required to claim those rights. Societies are enjoined, better yet, obliged to give those rights to the people. Otherwise, the quality of life is seriously compromised.

Stereotype: This "is an exaggerated [a generalization] belief associated with a category. Its function is to justify [and rationalize] our conduct in relation to that category."[36]

Segregation: "The policy or practice of separating people of different races, classes, or ethnic groups, as in schools, housing, and public or commercial facilities, especially as a form of discrimination."[37] Segregation is a form of discrimination that sets up spatial boundaries of some sort to accentuate the disadvantage of members of an out-group. For instance, segregation in the United States made it harder for many blacks (and other minorities) from getting good education, and to earn a good living. It also made access to life's amenities difficult, if not impossible, for many people in the 1960s and before that.[38]

By the same token, Osu riots and Osu/Diala segregation may have prevented some communities in Igboland from developing as rapidly as they should. That's why the system should be abolished.

What is wrong with the System?

The Osu caste system encourages segregation and violates the victim's human and civil rights. As noted earlier, the "Universal Declaration of Human Rights (UDHR)" is the main document that guarantees fundamental rights to human kind around the world. Yet, one of the basic problems facing the world today is how to preserve human rights in many societies.

The system discourages intimate love relationship and prohibits inter-marriages between the "Diala" and the "Osu." The Osu is thus expected to marry only within the group-a principle of endogamy that requires that marriages take place within the same group.[39, 40] Any Diala that goes contrary to this unwritten rule is usually ostracized. In some communities, such as Oruku community in Nkanu East Local Government area of Enugu State, any "Diala" that associates with an "Osu" pays a fine.

In Oruku community the Osu operate their own village market and it is often difficult for community to appoint an Osu to any position of authority in the local churches.[41] The Osu system is a form of discrimination and prevents freedom of association and the stigma associated with the system is unbearable because it is an ascribed status. As Arthur Schopenhauer (1788-1860) notes, "Suffering which falls to our lot in the course of nature, or by chance, or fate, does not seem so painful as suffering which is inflicted on us by the arbitrary will of another."[42] There is no justification for the continued practice of the Osu caste discrimination that divides the Igbo nation.

A Voice of Reason

The system is politically unpalatable in the Igbo society, as very few Diala want to participate in the discussion of the Osu problem. It occurs among people of the same heritage, within a family, and among people with the same skin pigmentation. The supporters of the system are hiding under the guise of culture to perpetuate discrimination. Why did the ancestors create the system?

Every normal person would like to live in harmony with others; and every reasonable person would prefer to be loved rather than to be hated. Some of the benefits of true democracy are fair and equitable treatment, justice, and freedom of association. (Some would argue that if people are free to associate, they should equally be free to disassociate). But these principles are not possible in a place where some sections of the society are treated like sub-human beings. Voices of reason and the Bible affirm the equality of human being! People should always endeavor to respect the rights of others: "All human beings are born equal and imbued by their creator with inalienable rights." But the Osu discrimination is not making this possible in Igboland!

Discrimination breeds discord that is detrimental to community development. As Anwar Sadat notes "He who cannot change the very fabric of his thought will never be able to change [the Osu] reality, and [the society] will never, therefore, make any progress."[43] The irony of the system is that the Diala who abhors racial discrimination in the United States and other parts of the world would not openly criticize the Osu practice. Is this not hypocrisy?

Because of the nature of the problem some people in Igboland believe that any person who speaks against the system could be an Osu. A friend of this author warned him that the public would think he is an Osu for writing on the "sensitive" Osu caste system in Igboland. And some would ask "If you were not an Osu, would you allow your son or daughter to marry an Osu?" Another person asks, "Do you think you can change the Igbo culture?" Although the questions were upsetting, this author mildly told the individuals that at this age in our civilization nobody would have any control over the person his or her children would marry.

Conclusion

This book will discuss these issues as they relate to the Osu caste discrimination. And this book will have achieved its main objective even if it can only prompt serious social discussion on the issue, change the mindset of the diehards, and initiate some social reforms. Therefore, everyone reading this book should look closely at the Osu caste system and join hands to dismantle the barrier to human relation and social progress.

Chapter 1
Notes and References

1. John Dewey: Experience and Education. New York: A Touchstone Book-Simon and Schuster, 1997 (first published in 1938)

2. Elizabeth Isichei: Igbo Worlds: An Anthology of Oral Histories and Historical Descriptions. Macmillan, London, England, 1977

3. Igbo Studies Association: (n/d) (www.igbostudies.com/information.htm) accessed 2001. The population of the Igbos is more than that of Norway, Switzerland, Denmark, Belgium, and Luxembourg combined. Also see *Uzoma Onyemaechi:* "Igbo Culture and Socialization" (Essay collated by The University of Michigan, Ann Arbor (accessed September 2001)

4. Finkelstein, et. al (1971)

5. J. Lofland and Lofland (1984). Analyzing Social Settings. Belmont, CA: Wadsworth.

6. Ronald J. Chenail (December 1995). "Presenting Qualitative Data". The Qualitative Report, Volume 2, Number 3. Also see Online: http://www.nova.edu/ssss/QR/QR2-3/presenting.html (accessed January 25, 2007)

7. The Eastern Regional government of Nigeria (1956): The Law promulgated to outlaw the Osu system by the then Eastern Regional government of Nigeria in 1956.

8. Sebastian Mbaonu Obi: How to Solve the Osu Problem. Owerri, Nigeria: Agape Edu Resources, 1994.

9. Kemjika Anoka: "Osu Across Beliefs;" Owerri: Outreach, July 28, 1991.

10. Victor E. Dike—"The Caste System in Nigeria, Democratization and Culture: Socio-political and Civil Rights Implications;" www.afbis.com, June 13, 1999.

11. Victor E. Dike—'The Osu Caste System in Igboland: Discrimination Based on Descent.' Paper Presented to the UN Conference—Committee on the Elimination of Racial Discrimination (CERD) Sixty-first session, Geneva (8-9 August 2002)

12. Jude Ezeala: Lecture at Fed Polytechnic; Nnekede, Owerri, Jan 18, 1992

13. Chinua Achebe: Things Fall Apart. New York, London: Anchor Books—Doubleday, 1959; also see Chinua Achebe: *No Longer At Ease* (2nd ed.) London: Heinemann, 1982

14. Encyclopedia: Columbia University Press Online: "Caste" ; accessed April 3, 2006

15. Britannica Online: See "Caste;" November 17, 1997.

16. The United Nations: Article 1 of the Universal Declaration of Human Rights

17. Lectric Law Library-Lexicon on Right: See Human Rights

18. American Heritage English Dictionary: Definition of "Culture;" accessed April 12, 2006

19. Neil J. Smelser: Sociology. Prentice-Hall, Inc., 1981, p.175

20. Villa Borsig Workshop Series (1999) on "Culture"; the culture of a people determines their way of life.

21. See: http://wordnet.princeton.edu/perl/webwn?s=discrimination—on Discrimination; accessed April 3, 2006

22. See: http://youthink.worldbank.org/glossary.php—on Discrimination; accessed April 3, 2006

23. The Encyclopedia Americana: International Edition 1999

24. The United Nations Publications (1949): XIV, 3, 2, for the main types and causes of discrimination.

25. The Encyclopedia Americana: International Edition:—Grolier—Vol.6, 1999 pp.768-776—also vol.14, 1999, pp.552c-552h.

26. Neil J. Smelser: Sociology. Prentice-Hall, Inc., 1981

27. Gordon W. Allport: The Nature of Prejudice (25th Anniv Edition; Addison-Wesley Pub. Company, 1979)

28. See: wordnet.princeton.edu/perl/webwn—"Bias" (accessed April 12, 2006)

29. See: The Webster New Collegiate Dictionary (1980), p.105

30. See: http://myweb.tiscali.co.uk/temetfutue/glossary/glossaryC.htm—Civilization; accessed April 3, 2006

31. See: The Webster New Collegiate Dictionary, 1980

32. See: The Universal Declaration of Human Rights (UDHR)

33. See: The Lectric Law Library-Lexicon on Right: accessed 2000—www.192.41.4.29/def2/q167.htm

34. Eleanor Roosevelt: www.americarhetoric.com/speeches/eleanorroosevelt.htm "The Struggle for Human Rights;" accessed 12/10/04

35. Post Express: See Claude Ake (Feb 3, 2000)

36. Gordon W. Allport: The Nature of Prejudice (25th Anniv. Edition), Addison-Wesley Pub. Company, 1979

37. See: *American Heritage English Dictionary*: On **"Segregation"** (accessed, April 12, 2006)

38. Mark Silverman: "Segregation too Costly to Ignore;" The Detroit News, Jan 14, 2002

39. J. S. Murthy: "Restorative Justice and India's Caste System." The New World Outlook: The Mission Magazine of the United Methodist Church, July-August 1999

40. Dodie V. Sarchet-Waller: "The Caste System: From the Beginning until Now." The New World Outlook: The Mission Magazine of the United Methodist Church, November 19, 1996

41. Tobs Agbaegbu: "Moves to Stop Slavery in Igboland." NewsWatch, Volume 31, Number 1, January 12, 2000

42. Arthur Schopenhauer (1788-1860): He notes 'The Suffering which falls to our lot in the course of nature, or by chance, or fate, does not seem so painful as suffering which is inflicted on us by the arbitrary will of another.'

43. Anwar Sadat (as cited in Stephen R. Covey: The 7 habits of Highly Effective People, 1989)

2

The Origins of the Osu Caste System: Some Mythological Explanation

Human beings are created equal, but their experiences are different. Life has been rough for some people, while others have been happy. But naturally, life has the same meaning for everyone; but the Osu absurdity has altered the meaning of life for the victims. Thus this section focuses on the origins of the system.

Who is an Osu?

There are various narratives as to the origin of the Osu caste system in Igboland. Studies have extensively documented the history of the Igbo people, but less work has been done in the area in discourse. For instance, Elizabeth Isichei[1] gives an excellent account of the history of the Igbo people from the dawn of their history up to 1973 and Victor Uchendu[2] examines the Igbo culture and its social system. Ogbau and Emenanjo[3] deal with varied aspects of the Igbo culture, including its language and dress while Njoku and Eberegbulam[4] discuss the rites performed in Igboland. These rites include, but not limited to, the rite of wearing cloths (Ima Akwa), the rite of circumcision, and the rite of Igba Mgba (wrestling).

Chinua Achebe[5] vividly describes the plights of the Osu (or outcasts). Although, the precise time the Osu system came into being is not certain, it is believed that the ancient system has been around for more that six Centuries. Who is an Osu? As noted earlier, the Osu is an "outcast"-a person whose ancestors were sacrificed or dedicated to the local deity in the Igbo community to appease the gods. The Osu system is a societal institution borne out of a primitive traditional belief system colored by superstition. As Things Fall Apart notes, an "Osu" is:

... A person dedicated to a god, a thing set apart—a taboo forever, and his children after him. He could neither marry nor be married by the freeborn. He was in fact an outcast, living in a special area of the village, close to the Great Shrine. Wherever he we went he carried with him the mark of his forbidden caste—long, tangled dirty hair. A razor was a taboo to him. An Osu could not attend an assembly of the freeborn, and they, in turn, could not shelter under his roof. He could not take any of the four titles of the clan, and when he died he was buried by his kind in the Evil Forest. How could such a man be a follower of Christ?[6]

Before the coming of Christianity to Igboland, people had the belief that the gods were very powerful. And they had found answers to some (if not most) of their problems in various gods and in traditional religion. And the people believed that the gods could wreck havoc in the society if they were not happy. The religious explanations to their problems were handed down from generation to generation in the form of myths. A myth is a story about the gods that sets out to explain why life is as it is.[7]

Oral Stories

There are many oral stories as to how the system originated in Igboland. In most cases, oral sources are central to the study of history in Igboland, and, in fact, in other parts of Nigeria (and Africa). In topics where written documents are limited, such as the issue in discourse, oral information and observation is a more convenient source of information. Some scholars appear uninterested in the subject for fear of being branded an Osu.

Over the years various mythological explanations have been given to explain how people were converted to Osu and how human beings were offered to the gods as sacrifice to appease them. In the primitive era almost everybody believed that the Osu belongs to the gods and that they would serve (performing various and make offerings to the gods) to give them powers to protect the community from evil forces. It is not only in Igbo culture that myths exist—there are many examples in other parts of the globe of the ways that people dramatized their myths of the processes of nature.

There are stories of the Greek gods of Zeus and Apollo, Hera and Athene, Dionysos and Asclepios, Heracles and Hephaestos, and others. However, around 700 B.C, Homer and Hesiod documented some of the Greek mythology. Before Christianity showed up in Norway, people believed that Thor (their god) rode across the sky in a chariot (with hammer) pulled by two goats. And when Thor swung his hammer it made thunder and lightning. Thus the word "thunder" in Norwegian—"Thordn" means Thor's roar.[8]

Stories have it that in the past the titleholders (the custodians of traditional belief systems of the Igbos) could offer intricate rituals to transform a Diala into an Osu. Some of the ancestors of the present-day Osu were converted to the absurd Osu status this way. But with Western influence, this ritual is no longer in practice.

In some communities, after being dedicated to a deity, a small part of the ear or fingers of the Osu convert is removed as identification.[9] It should be emphasized that people are not today quite dedicated to the gods. Strangely, in 1988 a woman from Onyohor in Igbo-Ekiti Local Government Area of Anambra State dedicated her daughter to the god of the Efuru Shrine to appease a powerful deity.[10]

You may have probably heard that the Osu were (some still are) confined to living at the edge of town near the Market Square so as to bear the brunt of any misfortune that might befall the community. (There is some cluster of the Osu living among the Diala in some villages). This gives the Osu a feeling of inferiority complex that has continued till today. In fact, some people think that the "Osu" is "pseudo-humans." But the reality is that they are human beings like every one of us! The various myths surrounding the system tried to offer the people some explanations for something they could not understand.

In the past, those captured in local wars (or kidnapped during community raids) are automatically converted to "Osu."[11,12] Also, a non-Osu could become an Osu by simply running into the home of a Shrine.[13] And in the past, to evade the wrath of the community, a criminal could knowingly convert to Osu by hiding in the shrine of a deity.[14] In some Igbo states (Ossomari and Arondizuogu) wars were sometimes fought with the intention of procuring captives and slaves. Some of the ancestors of the present-day Osu acquired their status this way. Presently, one could become an Osu through inheritance and marriage.[15,16,17] The system is a sad reminder of the indigenous religious historical past of the Igbos. It is thus 'an offshoot of the indigenous religious practice of the Igbos;' it "finds rationalization in Igbo religious beliefs and dogma."[18]The system is not a Pan-Igbo affair; it is not found "West of the Niger." [19]

As noted earlier, before Christianity came to Igboland some societies tended to punish their criminals by selling them into slavery. During the slave trade the Aros went into the evil forest to "liberate" the Osus who were thrown away to die for some alleged capital offences and then sold them into slavery. But 'the intelligent ones', who were sent back to their communities were planted as surrogates to serve the interest of the Aros.[38] In some cases parents were forced by "poverty and hunger" to get rid of their never-do-well children. During this era human (animal-goat) offerings to the gods was common and slaves were often used for this purpose. Some people were reportedly buried with the dead ruler of Igbo Ukwu.

With the abolition of slave trade (1807) the loss of external outlets for the sale of slaves led to an unprecedented escalation of the practice of using human beings for sacrifice. About forty slaves were used for human sacrifices at the death of Obi Ossai of Aboh, in 1845.[20]

There was (and still) a strong Igbo belief that the spirits of the ancestors keep a constant vigil over the people. As noted earlier, traditional religion was highly practiced by the traditionalists and the spirits of the all-important ancestors were worshipped through the gods or deities in the form of streams, rivers, lakes, caves, mountains, trees, animals, and the spirits of famous ancestors. The streams and rivers were seen as the homes of the gods and other spirits.[21] The gods were perceived (and some people still believe) as the bridges between the people and their life and that the gods could be appeased to protect the people.

Like other forms of oppression, such as racism, etc, *Osuism* thrives on the fertile ground of ignorance. As noted earlier, some of the deities are believed to be very powerful and therefore should be attended with intricate religious rituals in their shrines. The service for the gods entailed many arduous rituals. The practice lingered by delegating the service to the slaves. Thus, the slaves and their descendants are the properties of the gods. According to oral history those who served the gods were unjustly assigned the Igbo pejorative name of Osu, Ume, or Ohu arusi.

The Osu was originally regarded with "respect and honor" apparently because they were the property of the gods. They were not many in number in the early times; but as their numbers expanded the status deteriorated dramatically (in the nineteenth century). This show of respect for those who attended to the shrines transformed into social ostracism. They became "outcasts, feared and despised" and abhorred.[22]Another version noted that the advent of organized religion was said to have caused the social conditions of the Osu to deteriorate. When the Missionaries destroyed the shrines and the objects of worship and sacrifice, those that served the shrines remained the only visible link to the gods, shrines or the oracles and, thus, they fell out of favor.

There was another mythological explanation to the origin of the system and the struggle between good and evil. An old man told some children who were gathered with him around a camp fire during the *Harmattan* period how a group of traditional elders ganged up to sacrifice one of their own to the gods so that the gods would intervene when catastrophes loomed in the community. The story noted that his father told him that there was an agreement among the persons at the meeting. And, they swore in the name of the gods and on the *Ofor* that nobody would disagree with their final decision. (The *Ofor* is the bible for those who hold traditional Igbo beliefs.) If the powerful gods were made unhappy, they would not prevent evil to befall the community.[23]

The person who was later chosen to attend to the shrines did not know that he was the person that would be selected to perform the task of serving the gods. When the man was selected for sacrifice to the deities he jumped up from his chair and cried, as he knew what his status would become in the community. And a series of rituals and offerings of palm wine, goats, cola nut, etc, followed to transform the Diala to an Osu. The community built a hut for him at a market square, because in many Igbo communities the gods are usually located near the market. The Osu lived on the charity of the people in return for the performance of various services. Their descendants have inherited the "Osu" status.

This book rejects these reasons for sacrificing human beings to the gods to protect other human beings. Why would human beings sit idly by waiting for the gods to intervene while catastrophes such as drought or plague loomed? They should have prevented chaos and evil by doing what is right instead of taking human life or causing others pain and anguish. Ignorance and misconceptions color these multifaceted oral explanations of the reasons for the ancient Osu caste system that has caused an untold misery in Igboland.

Greek philosophers attempted to prove those similar mythological explanations to nature. For instance, the stories of how 'Thor-one' of the most important of the *Norse* gods, would swing his hammer to make thunder, lightning, and rain, were discounted or not trusted.[24] The Osu caste discrimination has no place in Igbo society at this stage in its civilization. Therefore, the campaign to dismantle the ancient system should begin today!

The Ancient System in Contemporary Igbo Society

When Christianity came to Igboland the Osu practice was already established. The Osu group thought that the arrival the Europeans could change their condition, as they were the first to embrace Christianity and Western education. The Europeans attempted to change the indigenous value systems and religious practices of the people. But they had not the necessary resources to radically transform the indigenous Igbo society, particularly the Osu system.

The system persists in parts of South Eastern Nigeria, including Nanka, Agolo, Ifite Ora village in Nawgu town, Akpu village, Abagana, and some part of Nnewi, all in Anambra State. It is also prevalent in Ukwu Ube (Nkwerre LGA), Imo State, and some parts of Mbaise.[25] The people of Umuaka (Imo State) categorize one of its Old Ten villages (Obinwanne formerly Amafor) "Osu." The people of Umuode in Nkanu East Local Government (Enugu State) are believed to be the descendants of Osu, and like in other areas, the rest of the communities in Oruku (Umuchiani and Onuogowu) have limited social interactions with them.

In Awka it is believed that the people of Amawbia-Awka are strangers and that gives them the derogatory and inferior Osu status. Previous inter-communal crisis is painful reminder of the problem in the area. In Ngo Village, Igboukwu, Anambra State, the people are daily grappling with the contradictions of the Osu and Diala divide. The people of Umu Ezeoruizu (kindred) in Akama are today bona fide Osu even though their great grandfather was a titled man who resided at Akama's obi. Iruowelle (Ihuowelle), the most populous section of Ngo Village, Igboukwu, is said to have a preponderance of Osu for a variety of reasons.[26]

In some places, such as Arochukwu, the traditional base of the old slave merchants, the Osu issue is not explicit because both the Amadis (freeborn) and the non-Amadis (settlers) live in harmony and inter-marry. But only Amadis are in-charge of "Ibinukpabi"—their ancestral deity—otherwise known as the "Long juju". The Osu system has caused communal clashes in the clans of Umuawuka and Emii in Owerri LGA, Imo State.[27,28] In Ifakala Community in the 1980s a water project was abandoned because the Diala complained that the project was 'located on Osu land.'[29] It is also practiced in Amano Okigwe and in Ama-Achara, Umuahia. The Osu caste discrimination, which is an Internal Apartheid, is virtually alive in every Igbo community.

The Osu Caste Discrimination: Internal Apartheid?

The Osu system, as noted above, besets Igboland, and sometime the government is part of the problem. In Enugu State, Mr. Maurice Ede (Commissioner for Special Duties), was allegedly dismissed because he protested the way the Enugu State government handled the Osu crisis in Oruku community (Maurice Ede is from Umuode). No matter their social status the local churches would hardly appoint the people of Umuode to positions of responsibility. This class ostracism is operated in such a manner that any person from the other side of the community who associates with any person from Umuode pays a fine of about N1000 (one thousand). Because of this the people of Umuode operate their own local market different from the Eke-oruku market owned exclusively by Umuchiani and Onuogowo. The people of Umuode have waged wars against this system (about five major conflicts since 1995) and many lives have been lost and properties destroyed.[30]

In the past, some people would refrain from dinning with or drink from the same water-well or touching the Osu for fear of being contaminated. During this period the Diala would not buy whatever the Osu merchants had for sell in the local market. This behavior is similar to what happened in the United States between 'Whites' and 'Blacks' during the Civil Rights struggles where they drinking from different public fountain.[31]

In Umuaka community (Imo State) the lower caste groups that are scattered in many kindred are given the pejorative Igbo expression of 'ndi ejiri goro ihe' (meaning those who are sacrificial lamb to the gods). In Umuaka (as in some other places) those interested in politics are not getting support from the rest of the community. The system affects relationships of love between the Osu and Diala. And it is an abomination for the Diala to marry an "Osu." As in Umuode the "Osu" in Umuaka revolted against the system in the late 1980s. They physically assaulted a couple of women (the Diala) with the intention of transforming them to Osu and the Diala responded with counter forces. Over 60 of such incidents have been reported Imo State alone, since 1979.[32]

In Isi Ala Mbano, the Osu and Diala do not inter-marry, but they live together. In some communities the Osu is regarded as property of the Diala. It is common in those areas to hear of "Ndia bu ndi Osu anyi", which means they are our slaves. The implication of this is in some parts of Igboland an Osu is not permitted to attain the "Ezeship". For instance, in Amufie village in Enugu Ezike, Enugu State, an Osu is not allowed to ascend the throne of an "Onyishi", a sacred position for the eldest man in the community.[38]

In Alor Agu community near Nsukka, in Enugu State, there is a deity "Adere', which is powerful and feared by the people, and any family (or person) who offends the god "offers animals including human beings to the gods" to appease "Adere'. And in some communities, such as in Nsukka area, some people have died in the struggle to destroy some shrines in an attempt to discourage the worship of the "idols" that seem to promote the Osu caste system.[38]

Although this book takes a closer look at the solutions to the Osu problem later, it is appropriate to mention in passing that the issue cannot be resolved by subduing the oppressed with force. The riots that took place in Umuaka in the late 1980s and those of Umuode in the 1990s are cautionary tales of what might happen to some communities if the problem is not solved soon. Any person who thinks that they deserve their social condition should walk in their shoes to feel their pains. As Martin Luther King, Jr. notes:

> "There comes a time when people get tired ... tired of being segregated and humiliated, tired of being kicked about by brutal feet of oppression. We have no alternative but to protest." [33]

We may not know everything about why and how conflicts occur in societies, several studies show that inequality, human and civil rights abuse, absence of rule of law, discrimination and absence of freedom are among the major causes of social unrest in African societies.[34]

Frustration, according to psychology, breeds aggression and hatred and discrimination breed frustration and aggression. Thus as the great philosopher, Baruch Spinoza (1632-1677) notes, "He who conceives himself hated by another, and believes that he had given him no cause for hatred, will hate that other in return." And Philosopher Spinoza, who belonged to the Jewish community of Amsterdam, was excommunicated for heresy. He criticized established religion, as "he believed that Christianity and Judaism were only kept alive by rigid dogma and outer rituals." "He denied that the Bible was inspired by God down to the last letter."[35]

Conclusion

The primitive and uncivilized Osu practice is wrong because there is no difference between the man-made Osu (outcast) and Diala (freeborn). Any system that is against freedom of association, equity, and the protection of the basic rights of the people is unjust.

Everything we know, including the knowledge of rights and wrong, according to John Locke "Is an inference that we have drawn on the basis of our experience."[36] Any person who has experienced any form of discrimination would understand what the victims suffer. It is painful to be discriminated against because injustice diminishes the humanity of the victims. Thus, "An injustice unresolved ... burns a hole in the heart."[37]

Chapter 2
Notes and References

1. Elizabeth Isichei: A History of the Igbo People. New York: St. Martin's Press, 1976

2. Victor C—Uchendu: The Igbo of Southeast Nigeria. Chicago: Holt, Rinehart and Winston, 1965

3. F. Ogbau and E. Emenanjo: Igbo Language and Culture. Ibadan: Oxford University Press, ed., 1975

4. John Njoku and E. Eberegbulam: The Igbos of Nigeria: Ancient Rites, Changes and Survival. New York: The Edwin Mellen Press, 1990

5. Chinua Achebe: Things Fall Apart. New York: Anchor Books, 1959

6. Chinua Achebe: Ibid.

7. Jostein Gaarder: Sophie's World-A Novel about the History of Philosophy. New York: Berkeley Books, March 1996

8. Jostein Gaarder: (March 1996) Ibid.

9. Felicitas Aigbogun: See "Osu Caste System in Nigeria" (n/d)

10. NewWatch (Jan 2, 1989)

11. Elizabeth Isichei: Igbo Worlds: An Anthology of Oral Histories and Historical Descriptions. Macmillan, London, England, 1977

12. Sebastian Mbaonu Obi: How to Solve the Osu Problem. Owerri, Nigeria: Agape Edu. Resources, 1994

13. Francis Arinze: Sacrifice in Ibo Religion. Ibadan: Univ. Press, 1970

14. Obi: 1994 (Ibid.)

15. Victor E. Dike: "The Caste System in Nigeria, Democratization and Culture: Socio-political and Civil Rights Implications;" June 13, 1999

16. Victor E. Dike: 'The Osu Caste System in Igboland: Discrimination Based on Descent.' Paper Presented to the UN Conference (CERD) Sixty-first session, Geneva (8-9 August 2002)

17. Kemjika Anoka: "Osu Across Beliefs" (Owerri: Outreach, July 28, 1991).

18. Okenwa R. Nwosu: "Osu Caste System: A Cultural Albatross for the Igbo Society" www.nigeriaworld.com (June 19, 1999).

19. Elizabeth Isichei: (1977) Ibid.

20. Elizabeth Isichei: A History of the Igbo People. New York: St. Martin's Press, 1976

21. Elizabeth Isichei: (1976) Ibid.

23. Note: Oral stories—Information gathered by the author from Igbo elders

24. Jostein Gaarder: Sophie's World-A Novel about the History of Philosophy. New York: Berkeley Books, March 1996

25. Daily Independent: "*Osu* caste system: 21st Century absurdity in Igboland;" November 24, 2005

26. Okenwa Nwosu: See Epilogue: E-mail discussion (July 16, 2006)

27. Daily Sunray: (May 7, 1993)

28. Obi: (1994) Ibid.

29. NewsWatch: (September 18, 1989)

30. Tobs Agbaegbu: "Moves to Stop Slavery in Igboland;" NewsWatch, 12 Jan 2000. See also "Slavery in Igboland;" NewWatch, 12 Jan 2000

31. Neil J. Smelser: Sociology. Prentice-Hall, Inc 1981, p.175

32. Tobs Agbaegbu: Ibid.

33. Martin Luther King, Jr.

34. The United Nations Publications (1949): XIV, 3, 2, for the main types and causes of discrimination.

35. Jostein Gaarder: Sophie's World-A Novel about the History of Philosophy. New York: Berkeley Books, March 1996

36. David Wooten: An Introduction to the Political Writings of John Locke. London: A Mentor Book, 1993

37. Ellis Cose: "Forgive and Forge;" Newsweek, April 21, 1997, p.45

38. Nigerian Tribune (Jan 14, 2007); see Jude Ossai "Osu Caste in Igboland"

3

The Osu Caste Discrimination and Stereotype

The previous chapters show how the Diala avoids the "Osu;" and they identify some of the Igbo communities where the system is prevalent. This chapter deals with the associated "Osu" stereotypes.

How the "Osu" is perceived in Igboland

Prejudice breeds discrimination; and any person that discriminates against another person does not wish that person well. When this author was younger, he heard many strange stories about the Osu in his community. Some of them are similar to what is documented in *Things Fall Apart* (see Chapter 2). As noted earlier, there is a belief that the Diala avoids the Osu for fear that it would pollute, contaminate, and transform them into an "Osu."[1]

There is the belief that since the Osu is dedicated to the gods it is a taboo to socialize with them. Some myths have it that they are isolated because they are "dirty," "repulsive body odor," and that they "steal," "dishonest" and "lazy." The village dwellers believe that the deities are powerful and dangerous and that the spirit of the deities would haunt them if they associate with them. Others fear they the society would ostracize them. There is hardly any person of Igbo extraction who is not aware of one stereotype or another about the Osu, even if the person does not hold one.

Why the stereotyping and ostracism? Is the man-made Osu not a human being? Is the stereotype against an Osu real and justified, or is it simply "pictures in our heads"? There is no empirical evidence to support the assertions. Stereotyping is not new. Among the "White" in the United States, Africans, in error, are labeled lower class in mentality and manners. In a study conducted in the United States in the 1930s, Young lists stereotypes about the "Negroes:" that African-Americans have "emotional instability, [and are] lazy and boisterous."

The possession of stereotypes interferes with rational judgment. Some people invoke the stereotypes to justify behavior (prejudice and discrimination) against their fellow human beings. The stereotypes have made people feel that the Osu is not human and therefore discount the contributions they are making toward the development of their communities. The system is an insult to humanity!

Forces Governing Human Belief

Let's bring philosophy (that evolved in Greece about six hundred years before the birth of Christ) into this discourse. Philosophers have tried to find explanations to things that happen in Nature. As noted earlier, in the past, things were explained through myths. People behave the way they do for varied reasons. Some believe in Fate, Faith, and some are Superstitious.[2]

Some people read horoscope magazines and believe in astrology. This group believes in Fate because astrologers are said to claim that the position of the star affects people's lives. And others would consult the oracle before they embark on some projects, so as to foresee their fate (destiny—"the end result of the actions of life, either good or unpalatable"). Even some people would hinge the outcome of a war on the intervention of the gods or deities. In other words, the gods could make a society win a war or prevent calamity from befalling a community.

The fortuneteller would determine the person's action or predict the future. Those who believed in Fate would claim that certain occurrences (such as a black cat crossing your way, certain numbers) could bring bad luck, yet, others believe in Fatalism—the belief that whatever happens is predestined. This belief goes across generation and it is all over the globe. In fact, "the Greeks were great believers in Fatalism."[3] Those who are Superstitious believed that certain sicknesses are punishment from the gods or deities that were angry and not appeased. They continued to give offerings to the gods until they die; and others believe that prayer alone would help a sick person recover.

The word *Faith* has various uses and meanings, but we are going to narrow this definition down to religious contexts (that is concerned here). It is "complete trust or confidence" (that could be religious belief or doctrines) "without logical proof."[4] In some instances, "faith means a belief in the existence of a deity, and can be used to distinguish individual belief in deities from belief in deities within religion." Thus, if one believed in Islam, Christianity or Judaism, it is termed Faith. But if one believe in astrology, it is Superstition—"an irrational belief arising from ignorance or fear."[5]

So many people are superstitious and in one way or another, all these govern their lives. And such was rampant in the primitive era! Do you have better explanation? However, how does the discussion relate to the discriminatory Osu system?

Socialization and the Osu Caste Discrimination

The culture of the society determines to a certain extent how the people socialize or interact with each other. Socialization is "the process by which people learn the skills and attitudes relevant to their social roles."[6,7] In some societies the youths could address an elder by his or her first name, and in others one could be scolded for doing that. In Igboland the elders command great respect and reverence, but in the Western world (the United States, in particular) a youth could casually greet an elder (if at all) by his or her first name.

Through socialization some people have internalized the prejudice and discrimination against the Osu. One of the social distinctions an Igbo makes in their social status is that of Diala and Osu. As noted earlier, the Diala is free to acquire any traditional titles in the community if he has the resources, but an Osu does not have such freedom. An Osu has an incredible social barrier and the name is so abhorred to the point that the most painful social insult one could inflict on a Diala is to call that person an Osu.

The elders have passed down the myths about the Osu and the beliefs in the gods to the youths. The deity seems to be present in every part of the lives of the elders, even at this stage in our civilization. The forces of good and evil confront each other in the struggle to extricate the Osu from the shackles of the primitive system. Any person born Osu would remain so no matter how educated or rich the person could become. How would one feel if everyone in the community would not interact with you?

Social problems in Igboland are legion, but none is as painful as the Osu caste divide. This palaver is one of the major causes of disunity in the Igbo society today. It is relatively easier to comprehend the gulf between the "White" and "Black" in the United States or in South Africa (the differences in their skin pigmentation). But it is difficult to fathom the Osu caste discrimination among a people with the same skin color and language. Thus the sufferings foisted on any person by nature may not be as painful as those inflicted on one by the arbitrary will of another person. This system has affected the progress of the Igbo nation.

Culture and Social Progress

The Osu caste system is "a cultural albatross for the Igbo society" because it is an impediment to human relations and social progress.[8] It has been noted that the culture of a people affects their lives. And one could argue that the Igbo culture (custom and tradition) has influenced the Osu practice. Culture has earlier been defined, but it is appropriate to add that it is:

> [An] ... integrated pattern of human behavior that includes thought, speech, action, and artifacts. It is the customary beliefs, social forms, and material traits of a racial, religious, or social group. However, the durability and sustainability of the culture of a group, depends upon man's capacity for learning and transmitting necessary knowledge to succeeding generations.[9]

As Kluckhohn (1962) has stated, culture is a set of "definitions of reality"[10] held in common by people who share a distinctive way of life. Culture consists of many elements, which include values, norms, ideologies, and language. Culture is "a vehicle for individual expression."[11] The culture of a people affects their behavior because the culture of a people is internalized and transmitted to succeeding generations. The custom of a people is, in part, "a usage or practice common to many or to a particular place or class or habitual with an individual;" a "long-established practice considered as unwritten law." The tradition of a people is "an inherited pattern of thought or action (as a religious practice or a social custom."[12] The ancient belief has overshadowed the good traditions and customs and values of the people.

Despite the discriminatory and primitive Osu caste system the Igbo nation cherishes its customs and traditions. Their belief is their strength and weakness: their strength because it is an indispensable nexus with the past, and their weakness because some of them are dehumanizing and discriminatory. Again, this brings us to the theme of this book.

A society's heritage, values, and customs, in large part, determine its social progress. No society should preserve any aspect of its culture that hinders its sociopolitical and economic progress. Analysts have blamed the woes of Africa on naked colonialism, exploitation and slavery.[13] There is no doubt that the Colonial masters plundered the continent, but Africans have their blames too. But has Africa made any progress since the Powers left the shores of Africa? In some instances, the retrogressive culture and tradition of the people have retarded the pace of their development.

George Will, a columnist writing in the *Newsweek* notes that the culture of a people (customs, mores, traditions, values, institutionalized ideas) rather than just legal institutions and economic policies are agents of progress in a society. He mentioned that DeMuth (then head of the American Enterprise Institute) had argued that economic prosperity of Western Europe and North America could be linked their "culture." The spread of democracy, free markets, and information technology is not enough to rescue many nations "from the consequences of their cultural deficits." But "Such deficits although not incurable, are intractable."[14]

The culture of a people is important to them because it is an important variable in their progress. "Culture is to an organization" what "personality is to the individual."[15] It is possible that the slave culture of housemaid, master/servant relations, personal chauffeurs on low income and apprenticeships without remuneration in Igboland (Nigeria in general) have influenced the way the society perceives the people's human rights. At a period when the world is evolving into a global community, there should be no room for the Osu hatred and bigotry.

The discriminatory system runs contrary to Chinua Achebe's portrayal of Igbo culture in *Things Fall Apart*. The story of how Okonkwu visited Nwakibie "to pay his respects and also to ask for a favor"[16] with two pots of palm wine shows a lot about Igbo culture. In presenting the Cola-nut and pouring of libation to the ancestors, Nwakibie intones:

> We shall all live. We pray for life, children, a good harvest and happiness. You will have what is good for you and I will have what is good for me. Let the kite perch and the eagle perch too. If one says no to the other let his wing break.

An injustice done to one person affects another person; and an "Injustice anywhere is a threat to justice everywhere."[17] One who discriminates against another does not wish that person (or group) well. For the Igbos' to be truly become their brothers' keeper they should respect the human and civil rights of others.

Conclusion

The Osu caste discrimination is a serious problem facing the Igbo nation today. The forefathers of the Igbo nation were known for their righteousness, honesty and hard work. The system is a serious challenge to the society.[18] Let us join hands and abolish the evil practice in Igboland for fairness, freedom and justice!

Chapter 3
Notes and References

1. Igwebuike Romeo Okeke: The 'Osu' Concept in Igboland: A Study of the Types of Slavery in Igbo-Speaking Areas of Nigeria. Nigeria: Access Pub, 1986

2. Jostein Gaarder: Sophie's World-A Novel about the History of Philosophy. New York: Berkeley Books, March 1996

3. Jostein Gaarder: (March 1996) Ibid.

4. See: The Oxford Desk Dictionary and Thesaurus American Edition. Oxford University Press, July 1997

5. See "Superstition" wordnet.princeton.edu/perl/webwn (accessed April 3, 2006

6. Phillips Mayer: Socialization: The Approach from Social Anthropology. London: Tavistock, 1970

7. Neil J. Smelser: Sociology. Englewood Cliffs: Prentice-Hall, 1981, p.171

8. Okenwa R. Nwosu: Osu Caste System: A Cultural Albatross for the Igbo Society"—See www.nigeriaworld.com (June 19, 1999)

9. The Webster's New Collegiate Dictionary: Definition of culture, 1980,

10. Clyde Kluckhohn: Culture and Behavior. New York: Free Press, 1962

11. Gigi Bradford, Michael Gary, and Glen Wallach (editors): The Politics of Culture. N.Y: The New Press, 2000

12. Victor C—Uchendu: The Igbo of Southeast Nigeria. Chicago: Holt, Rinehart and Winston, 1965.

13. Daniel Chirot: Social Change in the Twentieth Century. Harcourt Brace Jovanovich Inc., NY, 1977

14. George F. Will: "The Primacy of Culture;" Newsweek Jan 18, 1999, p. 64

15. R.M. Kilmann, M.J. Saxton, and R. Serpa: "Issues in Understanding and Changing Culture; California Management Review, vol. 28, No. 2, 1986.

16. Chinua Achebe: Things Fall Apart. New York, London, Anchor Books, Doubleday, 1959; also see the Glossary

17. The Rev Martin Luther King, Jr.

18. Jerome Njikwulimchukwu Okafor: The Challenge of Osu Caste System to the Igbo Christians. Onitsha: Veritas Printing and Publishing, 1993

4

Global Perspective: Social Disparity, Prejudice, and Discrimination across Nations

One of the aims of this book is to raise awareness about the Osu caste discrimination. To achieve this purpose information about system should spread beyond the boundaries of Igboland. This chapter juxtaposes the Osu palaver with similar human relations issues around the world to give it a global picture.

Global Dimension of Discrimination

Some people might be familiar with racial discrimination in the United States[1,] the Apartheid policy in South Africa[2,] and the Caste System in India[3,] but not the caste system in Igboland. Thus when the world is discussing human rights violations the system is not mentioned. Giving the Osu discrimination a global perspective will give the world a glimpse of the nature of the system and what the victims suffer. No person can live fruitfully and happily with the diminutive Osu caste stigma!

Prejudice and discrimination is a global phenomenon. But nobody would choose to be discriminated against and be unhappy! Discrimination of any form is wrong. The ability to distinguish right from wrong lies in the people and guided by the ethos of the society. However, as Frank Murphy notes "… Discrimination in any form and in any degree has no justifiable part whatever in our democracy…. All residents of this nation … [are] entitled to all rights and freedoms guaranteed by the constitution."[4]

Each generation retells the sacred myths of the people. The crude and primitive domination and control of human beings by others has powered the Osu system and similar practices around the world. The ancient Greeks believed in consulting their famous gods of the oracle, Apollo, at Delphi to know their fate.

They believed that Apollo knew everything; including the future.[5]Thus slavery was an integral part of the ancient Greek society. However, slaves were used for many tedious domestic chores in ancient Rome before the 2nd Century BC. But most of the slaves were foreigners and prisoners-of-war.[6]

The practice of human enslavement did not go unchallenged. Plato was known to have opposed the enslavement of Greeks. Three great slave revolts took place during this period. Two of such revolts occurred in Sicily in 135-132 BC and104-101 BC and the rest took place in Italy around 73-71 BC.[7,8] However, those slaves would become free by being granted *Manumission* (freedom) by their owner, or they could buy their own freedom. And any child subsequently born to the slaves would become a free citizen. The slaves did not remain slaves from cradle to grave. But any person born "Osu" remains one from cradle to grave! As Shirley Chisholm notes '… All forms of discrimination are equivalent to the same thing—anti-humanism.'

Discrimination comes in many shades and colors. Some Africans distrust Europeans; and the "White" world seem to believe that all bad things are African. The Acquired Immune Deficiency Syndrome (AIDS) is erroneously believed by the "White" to have originated from Africa. And politics plays a role; Communists distrust those espousing democratic principles, etc.

Some of the discriminatory practices hinge on race, as in the United States, and the Apartheid policy of South Africa and the color-caste system in Guyana. The Osu caste system in Igboland, the Caste of India (Dalit of India are widely known as untouchables in India and other South Asian countries such as Nepal, Bangladesh, Pakistan, and Sri Lanka) are based on culture. The Burakumin of Japan constitute a sizeable percent of population in their respective countries also suffer social and economic discrimination arising from "untouchability" and descent and work based discrimination.[9] A *Dalit*, which means 'broken people', is a modern form of untouchable; they do the dirty works in the society. In New Internationalist, Narayanamma, a toilet cleaner in India says:

> "'In the rainy season,' the woman began, 'it is really bad. Water mixes with the'"—excrement—"'and we carry it (on our heads) it drips from the baskets, on to our clothes, our bodies, our faces. When I return home I find it difficult to eat food sometimes. The smell never gets out of my clothes, my hair. But this is our fate. To feed my children I have no option but to do this work."[10]

Other discriminatory practices are based on religion. For instance some Moslems distrust the Christians, and anti-Semitism (hostility toward or discrimination against the Jews) menaces the Jews who escaped extermination in Central Europe in the new State of Israel. The Jews, in turn, appear bent on exterminating the Palestinians.

Prejudice and discrimination caused Adolf Hitler's hatred for the Jews (and the atrocities his followers committed at the Auschwitz concentration camp) are still fresh in memory. Millions were murdered between the summer of 1941 and the end of Second World War in 1945. About two and a half million people (men, women and children, of Jewish descent) perished at Auschwitz in gas chambers and ovens. The genocide represented what Hitler had called the final solution of the Jewish problem.[11,12,13,14]

The peace treaty signed between Israel, Egypt, and Jordan has not solved the Middle East problem. The Arab/Muslim-Israeli conflict continues with violence between Muslims and Christians. The Hizballah based in Lebanon, the Hamas and Palestinian Islamic Jihad (the Palestinian groups) have continued to cause mayhem in Israel.[15] It is not certain what will happen with the recent Hamas' surprise victory in Palestinian parliamentary elections.[16]

The 'World Conference against Racism' in Durban, South Africa in 2001 denounced the apparent 'racial discrimination' against the 'Palestinians' and other inhabitants of 'Arab occupied territories' by Israel. (Zionism—the movement that promotes a Jewish State in Israel) that "is based on racial superiority." The former Israeli Foreign Minister, Shimon Perez, responded to the criticisms leveled on Israel when he said, "We are talking about human rights. The first human right is to remain alive, and Israel is in danger. We are exercising the most important human right" and fighting for survival.[17] They should find a better way to co-exist.

Tracing Group Disparity In Other Nations

"Superiority is always detested"—Baltasar Gracian

1) The United States and Racism

In the United States, racial discrimination was prominent in the Southern part of the United States before the American Civil War (1860-1865). "From the 1880s into the 1960s, a majority of American states enforced segregation through "Jim Crow" laws." Many states and cities could impose legal punishments on people for associating with members of the rejected race. The 'laws forbade intermarriage (it was 'unlawful for a white person to marry anyone except a white person') and business owners and public institutions kept 'black and white' separate.[18]

The so-called *Jim Crow* laws enforced segregation, with separate public drinking fountains for blacks and whites. Other minorities—Hispanics, Vietnamese,

Native Americans were (and are still) treated with disrespect.[19]Federal and State laws by the end of the sixties prohibit discrimination in all places. And the laws weigh heavily on any person or organization found guilty of discrimination. Still, discrimination persists because there remains discrimination in employment, housing and also in marriage.

As Shaw[20]notes,

> In the year 2000, race in America still has a powerful impact on life experiences. Race affects mortality rates of black babies, the quality of education of black children, where blacks live, how they interact with the police, the kind of employment opportunities or health care available to them—in short, life experiences from cradle to grave.

Thus, "Blacks" suffer discrimination, as the banks are much more reluctant to give loans and grants to black than to Whites.[21]The ill treatment of blacks (both the poor as well as the affluent), is seen in attitudes towards them. The Ku Klux Klan (KKK) and the 'Skin Heads and White Supremacy' is among the reminders of the hostility (discrimination and prejudice) against the minorities in the United States.[22,23]Like racial discrimination in the United States and the Apartheid South Africa, the Osu caste system in Igboland promotes an ideology of the supremacy.

2) Apartheid South Africa

The black race suffered discrimination in the former Apartheid South. Apartheid (white/black segregation) was the law of the land before 1994. During the period in South Africa, the English distrusted the Afrikaner and both are against the Jews. The three are opposed to the Indians, but all the four conspire against the native black South Africans.[24] Apartheid system was destroyed by the combination of internal and external pressures. We may recall that the election of Nelson Mandela in 1994 as the first black president of the country brought a closure to the Apartheid system.[25] If the Igbos were opposed to the repressive Apartheid system why has it been difficult to for them to destroy its own Osu Apartheid, which is as repressive, if not more, than the Apartheid system?

3) The Caste System in India

The Osu caste system is similar to the caste discrimination in India, but the international community does not know it. The caste system that has been part of the Hindu religion is believed to be around for nearly 3000 years.[26,27] The original caste system in India, Varna, came about when the Aryan-speaking nomadic groups migrated from the north to India in about 1500 BC. The caste is an indicator of social and economic disparity in India.[28] About 60% live in Uttar Pradesh, West Bengal, and Bihar, Andhra Pradesh, and Tamil Nadu states.

The Harijans (the unclean, the lowest of the low caste, outcast, or untouchables) perform the menial jobs in the society.[29,30] They (Harijans) and Chamars were formerly denied access to skilled jobs and landed property by virtue of their caste status. In India religious sanctions are used to impose an assignment of social hierarchy, which is impossible to escape, except of course, by changing one's religion. In January 2004, this author saw first hand the havoc caused by caste system when he visited Mumbai (Bombay) India to participate in the World Social Forum (WSF).

India became an independent nation in 1947. Mahatma Gandhi fought against the evils of the caste system until he was assassinated in 1948. In September 1932, Mahatma Gandhi began the struggle to "bring about a silent revolution in the structure" in India. He lamented that "untouchability" was "crushing the very soul of Indian religion and society." Mahatma Gandhi promised the poorest and most down trodden of the India's poor-the untouchables—that democracy would free them from their misery. As noted earlier, he continued to fight to "eradicate the practice he found so abhorrent" until his death in 1948.[31]

The strongest and most frontal attack on the system has been the Constitution of India adopted on November 26, 1949. The 1949 "Constitution guarantees the right of all its citizens to justice, liberty, equality, and dignity."[32] India has since been working assiduously to bridge the country's bitter political divides. Although prejudice still exists in the villages, currently, India's outcast holds high paying jobs. The lower caste could marry from other groups in the cities. Thus, discrimination is a global problem; but that does not make it right!

4) Disparity in other Nations

There are divisions in other nations across the globe. In Guyana, a color-caste system has produced a racially divided labor market. The Africans (blacks) are said to dominate the civil service, the professional positions, and industry. And Indians are known to control agriculture and small businesses.[33] In the Indian Andes in South America, linguistic and cultural characteristics provide the basis for discrimination. The Indio, like virtually everyone else in the region, is of mixed ancestry. And the Indio, unlike others, is "kept in his place" by his mode of dressing, his habits, etc.[34]

In Yemen, the Akhdam "the black skinned" (street-sweepers and beggars)-the lowest of the low Castes—are held at the bottom of the social and economic ladder. In Arabic, the word, Akhdam, means servants-Yemen's Akhdam "Out-Castes."[35] To some extent, their social position is similar to the "untouchables" of India. They are "despicably low that they are mostly shut out from the rest of society." "They are almost always kept at arms length, and any chance of social integration is next to impossible." [36]

For century's discrimination has isolated them from the mainstream of the society. Although their conditions have improved a little bit, they still suffer certain social stereotypes. The mainstream society considers them immoral, dirty and ill mannered. They are socially ridiculed; their plates are considered dirty. Others don't eat with them because they would say, "Don't eat with the Akhdam because worms come out of their plates."[37] The Akhdams are poorly educated and they do not reveal their social caste to outsiders for fear of being ostracized. And in Somalia the Midgan/Madhiban represents the outcaste of the "pure" the "noble."[38,39]

The 1999 conflict in Yugoslavia had ethnic and religious coloration. The Kosovars (the Moslem ethnic Albanians) demanded political autonomy from Yugoslavia, but Slobodan Molisevic crushed the people and their demand. However, the world did not allow the 'ethnic cleansing' to go unpunished, as the Serbs were bombed to submission.

The people's October 2000 revolution forced Slobodan Molisevic out of office. He was arrested and indicted on war crimes charges by the International Criminal Tribunal at The Hague.[40]But the man died in jail in March 2006. The massacre of the Chechens by Russia is another reminder of the prevalence of prejudice and discrimination all over the globe. The world turned a deaf ear to this unjust extermination of a group by Russia. The list of injustice around the globe can go on forever.

Conclusion

The world would be a better place if people of different tribal and religious groups could device ways to co-exit amicably with one another. Thus injustice, inequity, human rights abuse should not be tolerated anywhere in the globe. As Thabo Mbeki[41] notes ... We will be able to measure the distance we have traveled towards the accomplishment of these objectives by the degree to which we have succeeded to close the great racial divides which continue to separate our communities. The Igbos should eradicate the Osu caste system; but there is need for a global cooperation to tackle the problem.

Chapter 4
Notes and References

1 Jim Crow Laws: http://www.sju.edu/~brokes/jimcrow.htm (Jan 24, 2002); also see **The Economist:** The banks are more reluctant to lend money to blacks than to whites in the United States (July 10th 1993)

2."The History of Apartheid in South Africa": http://www-cs-students. stanford.edu/~cale/cs201/apartheid.hist.html (accessed April 13, 2006); also see *Justice Malala:* South Africa: Racism Runs Deep (South African: Sunday Times, August 30, 2000).

3. J.S. Murthy: "Restorative Justice and India's Caste System"—The New World Outlook: The Mission Magazine of the United Methodist Church (July—August 1999)

4. Justice Frank Murphy: United States Supreme Court (1940-1949), born April 13, 1890. See *The Columbia Encyclopedia*, Sixth Edition (Copyright 2006 Columbia University Press).

5. Jostein Gaarder: Sophie's World-A Novel about the History of Philosophy. New York: Berkeley Books, March 1996

6. Lesley Adkins and Roy A. Adkins: Handbook to Life in Ancient Rome. N.Y, Oxford: Oxford University Press, 1994

7. Lesley Adkins and Roy A. Adkins: Oxford University Press, 1994; Ibid.

8. John Madden: Slavery in the Roman Empire Numbers and Origins Ireland: Classics Ireland, vol.3, Univ. College Dublin, 1996

9. UNITED NATIONS (Press Release): Committee on Elimination of Racial Discrimination holds a Discussion on Discrimination Based on Descent (CRED 61st Session, August 8, 2002); also see *UNRISD:* The Social Construction of Race and Citizenship, 2001

10. Dalit Monitor: E-Newsletter of the Dalit Human Rights Monitoring Project of People's Watch-Tamil Nadu (April-May 2004).

11. Gordon W. Allport: The Nature of Prejudice (25th ed.). Addison—Wesley Publication, Company, 1979

12. **Neil J. Smelser:** Sociology. Prentice-Hall, 1981

13. **William L. Shirer:** The Rise and fall of the Third Reich: A history of Nazi-Germany, 30th Anniversary Edition (1960)

14. **Lewis** (1999)

15. **Time** (USA): Terrorist groups in the Middle East are out to destroy the State of Israel with the help of their allies (Feb. 28, 2000), p.22.

16. **BBC News:** "Hamas sweeps to election victory" (January 26, 2006)

17. **CNN.Com/World**: S. Africa trying to revive UN racism meeting (Durban, South Africa (September 3, 2001)

18. **Jim   Crow:** http://www.pbs.org/homecoming/jimcrowpop.html (Jan 23, 2002); and The Origin of "Jim Crow:" http://www.toptags.com/aama/docs/jcrow.htm (Jan 25, 2002); See also: Creation of the Jim Crow South: Segregation in the South http://afroamhistory.about.com/library/weekly/aa010201a.htm (Jan 25, 2002).

19. **Neil J. Smelser:** Sociology (Prentice-Hall, 1981)

20. **Theodora M. Shaw:** The Debate Over Race Needs Minority Students' Voices. The Chronicle of Higher Education, February 25, 2000, A72.

21. **The Economist:** The banks are more reluctant to lend money to blacks than to whites in the United States (July 10th 1993)

22. **Neil J. Smelser:** Sociology (Prentice-Hall, 1981)

23. **Bruno Bettelheim and M. B. Janowitz**: Social Change and Prejudice (New York: Free Press, 1964)

24. **Gordon W. Allport:** The Nature of Prejudice (25th ed). Addison-Wesley Publication, Company, 1979

25. **BBC News:** "1994-99 The Mandela Years" (June 14, 1999); also see BBC News: "Profile: Nelson Mandela;" June 1, 2004

26. Dodie V. Sarchet-Waller: "The Caste System: From the Beginning until Now;" The New World Outlook: The Mission Magazine of the United Methodist Church (19 Nov 1996)

27. J.S. Murthy: "Restorative Justice and India's Caste System" The New World Outlook: The Mission Magazine of the United Methodist Church (July—August 1999)

28. Ashwini Deshpande: "Does caste still define Disparity? A look at inequality in Kerala, India" (Post doctoral research fellow, Carolina Population Center, UNC Chapel Hill and Lecturer of Economics, Delhi School of Economics, Delhi, India (Southern Economic Association Meeting, New Orleans, November 1999)

29. Dodie V. Sarchet-Waller: (19 Nov 1996), Ibid.

30. J.S. Murthy: (July—August 1999), Ibid.

31. Ignatius Jesudasam: A Gandhi Theology of Liberation. New York: Orbis Books, 1984

32. J.S. Murthy: (July—August 1999), Ibid.

33. Ralph P. Premdas: "The Ethnic Conflict and Development: The Case of Guyana." In UNRISD: Social and Development News, No.13, Aut/Win 1995.

34. John Howard Griffin: "Beyond Otherness" (1979) essay on race. See also *Black Like Me* (Foreword by Studs Terkel); San Antonio, TX: Wings Press, 2004. *Black Like Me* was first published in November 1961)

35. Huda Seif: "The Accursed Minority: The Ethno-Cultural Persecution of Al-Akhdam in the Republic of Yemen: A Documentary & Advocacy Project;" Muslim World Journal of Human Rights, Volume 2, Issue 1, 2005

36. Shane Bauer: "The Akhdam: Living through Centuries of Inequality;" Yemen Observer Newspaper, March 19, 2005, Vol.111, Issue11

37. Dalit Monitor: E-Newsletter of the Dalit Human Rights Monitoring Project of People's Watch-Tamil Nadu (April-May 2004).

38. Dalit Monitor (Ibid)

39. Asha A. Samad (Anti-Slavery International): Sub-Commission concludes Debate on Prevention of Discrimination: Sub-Commission on the Promotion and Protection of Human Rights (55th session), 12 August 2003

40. CNN.Com/World: Milosevic move prompts aids pledge (June 29, 2001).

41. Justice Malala: South Africa: Racism Runs Deep. South African: Sunday Times, August 30, 2000

5

Ethical Dimensions of the Osu Caste Discrimination

This chapter deals with the ethical dimensions of the Osu caste system. We shall begin this chapter with a story that touches on the ethical dimensions of the system to introduce our readers to basic ethics as it relate to the issue.

The Osu Caste System and Human Behavior

Ethics is important for private and professional life. Analysts have been shoveling through the moral puzzles surrounding the Osu caste discrimination as the proponents of the system have reduced ethics to individual preference. Some people would perceive the word, Osu, to be too controversial to discuss, and thus, could change the topic whenever it pops up. But the system is hateful, devilish, and unethical and the stigma is unbearably dehumanizing and thus should be swept under the rug.

Ethics is a branch of philosophy concerned with rightness and wrongness of human behavior and its effects on society. It is often used interchangeably with morals that refer to human behavior and to formalized code of conduct. Ethics comes from the Greek word *ethos* and *morals* from the Latin word mores.[1] And they are relevant in the Osu controversy as they are concerned with people's thinking and actions. Ethics assumes that individuals have the ability to make informed choices about their actions or behavior.

The Osu caste system is real and the victims are suffering silently as they are subjected to inhuman treating simply for being born into the so-called Osu family.[2] Some people would pretend that the system does not exist; but it operates within their sub-conscious. In some communities 'you do not see it or touch it' yet people always verify people status before they or their siblings enter into any serious relationship of love.

Many lives have been ruined by the Osu caste discrimination. There are many other pathetic stories surrounding the system (in the book) but we shall begin with that of Agnes Nwachi as she narrated her Osu ordeals to a *Vanguard* reporter. Some people from her community, *Eru*, in Ebonyi State, tried to eliminate her and her family as they are classified "Osu", which is an outcast in *Igboland*. The Osu palaver forced them to leave their village in 1999, for *Badagry* (Lagos) via Cross River State.

But the issue would not go away; her husband, David Nwobu Nwachi, was murdered in Cross River state. Before they left their village (*Eru*) they were advised to perform a special type of 'fetish sacrifice' to the gods of the land, without which they would face some tragedies. On November 30, 2006, the family suffered another devastating blow when some people, whom she alleged were sent to eliminate them by the Osu proponents in their village (Eru), stormed their apartment in *Badagry*. They 'beat her to a state of coma and abducted one of her sons, Paul' when they could not find their father. And her daughter-in-law who was living with them was also 'beaten to a state of coma and left to die in a gutter.[2] What crime has this family committed to deserve such ill treatment?

Their ordeal was reportedly published in one of the national Newspaper in 2004, but did not receive any assistance from the police or the civil society. When the *Vanguard* reporter contacted the Lagos State Police Public Relations Officer on the issue, he noted that he was not aware of the incident, but promised to find out if such a thing really occurred.[2] Now, the family is scared of coming out in public and even going 'to the market' for fear that their assailants might get them. Therefore, Mrs. Nwachi is pleading to well meaning Nigerians and 'the international community' to save their 'souls.'

As noted in previous chapters (see Chapter 2) there are many other gory stories surrounding the Osu caste system in *Igboland*, such as the Osu crisis in *Oruku* community were the people of *Umuode* have been reduced to sub-human beings. These stories are just a glimpse of the trauma the Osu stigma is causing the victims. The system remains a challenge to the Igbo community. In some villages it is an abomination to have an Osu as a friend. The seriousness of the Osu caste system is seen in the fact that in the die-hard communities the *Diala* (freeborn) would not marry an Osu (outcast) 'even at gun point' and 'no matter how wealthy an Osu could be.'

Such people would prefer to remain single their entire life if marrying an Osu is the only alternative, because they cannot withstand the humiliation in their village for marrying an Osu.[3] Few *Igbos* would deny the fact that the Osu system is debasing human values in the society today. What has happened to respect for human life and basic social values? What would you do if you were one of the victims of the system? More often than not the proponents of the system would think that the end results and circumstances should determine and control their behavior. This perception is in line with the utilitarian teaching of John Stuart Mill[4] (see below) or the situational ethical preaching of Joseph Fletcher[5]that believes that 'no act in itself is good. Only love is good in itself.'[5]

Ethical Implications of the Osu Caste Discrimination

The stories of human rights violations surrounding the Osu caste system (see next chapter) raise some ethical questions. What are the justifications for the Osu system? There are other philosophical theories that could address the issue but ethical theories are more relevant.

Ethics (moral philosophy) is a fundamental part of the life in community, society, institutions, and professional roles. Ethics has been variedly defined as the study of ideal conduct; and the study of right and wrong in conduct.[6,7] It is a systematic reflection on and analysis of morality or recommending concepts of right and wrong behavior. Philosophers and Theologians (ethicists) who study ethics go extra mile in understanding morality and its implication in every day life.[1]

As we discuss the Osu caste discrimination we will become ethicists because we will apply ethical tools in analyzing its effect on the lives of the victims and society. There are two main areas of ethical analysis: Metaethics and *Normative* ethics.[8]And we shall briefly discuss them as they relate to the issue.

Metaethics[8]

It is important to discuss Metaethical theories here because we live in a pluralistic society where one person's basic moral belief and assumptions may differ from others. The term "meta" means 'after' or 'beyond'. Metaethics is the study of the origin and meaning of ethical concepts[8.] It tries to explore and discover reasons given by individuals for making a moral judgment in life. What reasons are valid when we try to defend something or an act we say is right? Is an act "right" because the society says it is "right" or do we believe that the act is "right"? Metaethics requires that we should be aware of our beliefs as they are influenced by our religion, philosophy, and culture (what we have been told or taught) and how they influence our feelings of what are rights and wrong. What are your sources of moral belief?

The two Metaethical approaches are: a) absolutism; and b) relativism.[8,9] Let us briefly discuss them as they relate to the Osu issue. *Absolutist Metaethical Theories* hinge on the notion that what is right is based on your source of knowledge that can be known to be always a truth. Sometimes religious teachings or beliefs are believed to be absolute truths because they are from the scripture or by intuition. In this case, people don't worry about the alternative because it is obvious their thinking or actions (such as discrimination) are right.

Relative Metaethical Theories hinge on the assumption that ethical questions are not known to be absolutely true or false.[8,9] For instance, some people are not certain what reasons they could give for discriminating against another person. And there are no true reasons to guide one on what is right or wrong on certain issues. Therefore, one person's morally right judgment could be another person's wrong judgment. What a person, a society or a group states is right can be defended against what another person, society, or group asserts. All is relative! Whether you are an absolutist or a relativist nothing makes a wrong action right!

Normative[8]

Normative ethics asks direct and concrete questions that are related to morality, such as what acts are morally right or wrong? What acts are morally praiseworthy or not? What values are morally good or bad for harmonious co-habitation or functioning of society or and welfare of individuals? For that people usually follow social norms, which are basic units of morality applied in normative ethical thinking. Normative ethics are divided into Deontological and Teleological theories; and they dictate that individual or group actions should be guided accordingly.

Deontological Theories: They hold that a person (or society) acts rightly when the person (or society) acts according to one's duties and rights and sense of responsibility. Here duties and rights are used to evaluate right a course of action. Most often the person who is identified with deontological approaches *is* Immanuel Kant (1724-1804). Kant believed that every person has inherent dignity and for that, one is entitled to respect.[9] Respect is given to people when they are not "used" to achieve other goals or 'consequences'. Right things are always guided by moral duties, responsibilities, and rights. Immanuel Kant believed that some actions are intrinsically immoral no matter how positive or how rational one might judge the action. The consequences of immoral actions are purely irrelevant.

The root word "Deonto" is "duties" in Greek; and they are known as 'MEANS' theories. Kant does not believe that you are really benefiting if you use a wrong action to achieve your consequence.[9]We have the duties, rights, and responsibilities to protect and respect our fellow human beings, and thus, should not discriminate against them in whatever way, including the descent-based Osu caste discrimination. The so-called Osu is a human being and human beings should always be treated with respect and with dignity.

And W.D. Ross[10] emphasizes *prima facie* (true, valid, self-evident, etc) duties, and argues that our duties are "part of the fundamental nature of the universe."[10] Another aspect of duties should discuss here is how duties arise. What are some of your commitments in a society or institution? Do you have an obligation to do what is right in your private and professional life? David Hume (1711-1776) reasoned or argued that since you 'receive the benefits of society' you thus 'ought to promote its interests.'[11] Human beings are interdependent; and there are reasonable expectations that we treat our fellow human beings humanely. And our duties and obligations give rise to a sense of responsibility.

Teleological Theories: They are concerned with consequences, utility, or usefulness. And utilitarianism is considered here. For utilitarianism (see Mill), an act is right if it is useful to bring about the best consequences. This approach, which is quite opposite of Kant's deontological approach, was first developed by Jeremy Bentham (1748-1832)[12] and John Stuart Mill (1806-1873)[13, 14]. The root word, "Telos" means "end" in Greek. The theory holds that the "END" justifies the means! However, what is the "end" or justification for the Osu caste discrimination? As Voltaire would say, "It is the duty of a man (or woman) like you to preferences, but not exclusions."[7]

What about Justice and Fairness?

We cannot talk about the Osu discrimination without mentioning justice. Let's cast back on Agnes Nwachi's story and situation. Injustice is among the issues in the Osu palaver. Justice has been defined in varied ways, but each of them is based on the fundamental idea of giving to each person his or her due.

John Rawls is known for his work on justice. His first principle of justice states that "Each person is to have an equal right to the most extensive total system of equal basic liberties compatible with a similar system of liberty for all". All people are perceived as equal and therefore deserve equal treatment under the law.[15] Rawls also defines "justice as fairness".[16] Justice is often perceived as an 'arbiter'. Justice is consulted when there are problems regarding what is rightfully due a person, institution, or society. And the duty of justice requires an equitable distribution of benefits and burdens.

There are three types of Justice (distributive, compensatory, and procedural): Distributive justice deals with comparative treatment of individuals in the allotment of benefits and burdens; compensatory justice concerns compensation for wrongs that have been done (it could apply to people who have been wronged in society because of past discrimination, etc); and procedural justice arise in processes that require ordering in a 'fair' manner.[16] The discussion of compensatory justice and costs,[17] which concerns compensation for wrongs that have been done (apply to people who have been wronged in society because of past discrimination, etc) is relevant here. Should the Osu caste victims be compensated by the society for the injuries the system inflicts on them?

What about Rights?

A right is a justified claim on others. The most influential early account of rights theory, John Locke[18] (1632-1704) argued that the 'laws of nature mandate that we should not harm anyone's life, health, liberty or possessions.' For him, these are our natural rights, given to us by God. The United States Declaration of Independence, authored by Thomas Jefferson, asserted that "all men ... are endowed by their Creator with certain unalienable rights ... among these are life, liberty, and the pursuit of happiness." These "rights" are "inalienable", which apparently means that I or any person cannot hand over my rights to another person, such as by selling me or another person into slavery.

Immanuel Kant's work is one of the most influential interpretations of moral rights. He maintained that everyone has a worth or a dignity that must be respected. As a moral principle Kant noted that humanity must always be treated as an end, not merely as a means. And to treat a person as a mere means is to use a person to advance one's own interest. But to treat a person as an end is to respect that person's dignity by allowing each the freedom to choose for him or herself. Immanuel Kant's principle is often used to justify both a fundamental moral right.[19] According to him "In law a man is guilty when he violates the rights of others. In ethics he is guilty if he only thinks of doing so."

Rights are stringent claims a person or group makes on society in general or on a specific individual or group. Has the Osu the rights to 'freedom' of 'association'? Has the Osu the right to ask for fair treatment? The rights (life, liberty, etc) of the Osu ought to be protected without excuses of culture or custom.

Conclusion

What role does this complex web of ethics (moral Philosophy) play in dealing with the subject matter? As we have seen "Critical Philosophy" plays an important role in the history of thought.[7] Thus, the application of human knowledge (the work of philosophers) 'to our social antagonisms' will help us deal with the complex and daunting Osu caste discrimination that remains a challenge to the

Nigerian democracy and Igbo community.[20] If the Igbo community wants to live together in harmony human values and the values[21] the community hold dearly should not be diluted or debased. People should respect one another and adhere strictly to the code of ethics and any person that goes contrary to the rules should be punished without fear or favor. They should start doing the right thing and not to sweep the Osu issue under the rug!

Chapter 5
Notes and References

1. Kant, Immanuel (1963). Lectures on Ethics; translated by Louis Infield. New York: Harper & Row; also see Kant, Immanuel. (1949). Critique of Practical Reason and Other Writings in Moral Philosophy (Lewis White Beck, ed.,). Chicago: University of Chicago Press; see also Frankena, J. (1973). Ethics; New York: Prentice-Hall; also see Taylor, P.W. (1975). Principles of Ethics: An Introduction. Encino, CA: Dickson Publishing Company; and see Thiroux, J.P. (1990). Ethics, Theory, and Practice (4th edition); New York: Macmillan

2. *Vanguard* (January 22, 2007); see Evelyn Usman—"Widow on the run, cries for help over caste system;" also see Victor E. Dike (2002). The Osu Caste System in Igboland: A Challenge for Nigerian Democracy. Kearney, NE: Morris Pub.

3. *Nigerian Tribune* (January 14, 2007); see Jude Ossai "Osu Caste in Igboland"

4. Mill, John Stuart (1991). Utilitarianism; In Collected Works of John Stuart Mill (ed., J.M. Robson 1991); London: Routledge and Toronto, Ont.: University of Toronto Press

5. Fletcher, Joseph (1966) Situation Ethics; Philadelphia, PA: Westminster

6. Aristotle. Nicomachean Ethics. Translated W.D. Ross (1980); Oxford: Oxford University Press

7. Durant, Will. (May 1976). The Story of Philosophy: The Lives and Opinions of the Great Philosophers. New York: Pocket Books

8. *Internet Encyclopedia of Philosophy* (Ethics) http://www.iep.utm.edu/e/ethics.htm#H1 (accessed April 2, 2007).

9. Kant, Immanuel. (1949). Critique of Practical Reason and Other Writings in Moral Philosophy (Lewis White Beck, editor); Chicago: University of Chicago Press

10. Ross, W.D. (1935). The Right and the Good. Oxford: The Clarendon Press

11. Hume, David. On suicide; in Gorovitz, S. et al. (ed., 1976); Moral Problems in Medicine; Englewood Cliffs, NJ: Prentice-Hall; Hume, David. A Treatise of Human Nature (1739-1740) (David Fate Norton, Mary J. Norton, edited 2000); Oxford; New York: Oxford Univ. Press

12. Bentham, Jeremy (1789). Introduction to the Principles of Morals and Legislation; In The Works of Jeremy Bentham (edited by John Bowring)

13. Mill, J.S. (1939). On liberty; The English Philosophers from Bacon to Mill (Edwin A. Burtt, editor) New York: Random House

14. Bentham, J., & Mill, J.S. (1939). The English Philosophers from Bacon to Mill (Edwin A. Burtt, editor). New York: Random House

15. Rawls, John. (1971); Theory of Justice. Cambridge: Harvard Univ. Press

16. Rawls, John. (2001). Justice as Fairness: A Restatement Cambridge: Harvard University Press

17. Amdur, Robert (May, 1979). "Compensatory Justice: The Question of Costs" In Political Theory, Vol. 7, No. 2, pp. 229-244

18. Locke, John (1963). Two Treatises (edited by Peter Laslett); Cambridge: Cambridge University Press

19. Kant, Immanuel. (1949). Critique of Practical Reason and Other Writings in Moral Philosophy (Lewis W. Beck, ed.,). Chicago: Uni. of Chicago Press

20. Dike, Victor E. (2002). Ibid

21. MacIntyre, Alasdair (1984) After Virtue (2nd ed.,); Notre Dame: Notre Dame University Press; also see Raths, L.E.; M. Harmin & S.B. Simon (1979). Values and Teaching (2nd ed.), Columbus, OH: Merrill

6

The Osu Caste Discrimination: Human and Civil Rights Implications

The Osu caste system encourages segregation and thus infringes on the people's human rights. 'Expansion of freedom' is essential for human interaction and social development. This chapter deals with the human and civil rights implications of the system.

The 1956 Law and Lack of Implementation

Aristippus, one of the pupils of Socrates, believed that the aim of any person in life is to achieve the highest happiness: "The highest good is pleasure" and "the greatest evil is pain."[1] And pleasure could be defined variedly, given people's different values. However, "The quality of our lives should not be measured only by our wealth, but by also our freedom."[2] The Osu system is causing a lot of displeasure to the victims. What is life if there is no freedom?

Could real happiness be achieved if there are no laws to protect human rights? The 1956[3] law promulgated to outlaw the system by the then Eastern Regional government of Nigeria was not effective. Without appropriate laws the Osu discrimination would continue to abridge the freedom of those subjected to it. Nobody has been tried or convicted under the law and the victims are without legal recourse. The proponents of the Osu system appear ignorant of the Abolition of Slavery Act of 1806.

The administration of late Sam Mbakwe in Imo State, banned the Osu caste system, but that did not stop the practice. (Some would argue that Sam Mbakwe did that because was one himself). And the military governor of old Anambra State, the late Air Commodore Emeka Omeruah attempted to discourage the Osu practice by destroying the Efuru deities in Ukehe in Igbo-etiti Local Govern-

47

ment Area with bulldozer. A paramount ruler in Enugu-Ezike, Igwe Simeon Itodo has noted that the Osu system should be cast to the dust bin of history as all men are equal before God. And a law Professor, Celestine Abugu, from Amachalla, Enugu-Ezike (Igbo-eze Local Government Area of Enugu State) opined that the system is not only dehumanizing, but outdated and should be discarded.[17]

What is the reason for the 'needless man's inhumanity' to his fellow human being? As John Lennon notes, "Living is easy with eyes closed." The system has many impacts that are classified into Human Rights, Civil Rights, and Political Implications. Let's begin the discussion with the human rights implications.

1). Human Rights Implications

The story of the human race, from age to age, is full of the struggle to enjoy certain fundamental rights, including freedom from inhuman treatment and slavery, discrimination, freedom of thought, assembly and association and others that are "reasonably justifiable in a democratic society."[4]Any culture (tradition and custom) that abridges a people's freedom of association violates their human and civil rights. As mentioned earlier, the Osu system has created a rigid distinction of social status in Igboland—between the Diala and Osu (Ume). And this has caused a debilitating psychic pain to the group subjected to the system.

Human rights constitute the very foundations of democracy. And one wonders how democracy would thrive in a society in which such a discriminatory system exists. Freedom and liberty to pursue happiness are basic human rights; and they drive social struggles throughout the history of mankind. When a group is enslaved they lack freedom; and where there is no freedom there is obviously no happiness. The protection of human and civil rights of the people is issues of concern to those running the affairs of Nigeria. If not, why should they remain silent in the face of such tyranny? And the plethora of human rights organizations in the society is not doing enough to tackle the system.

The article in *Punch* of January 10, 1996[5] where a young man on his national youth-service duties in Imo State, was discouraged from dating a beautiful young lady because she was an Osu. The young man (not Igbo) broke the good news that he found a new lover to his close friend. But this person who happened to know the social background of the girl (an Osu), instead of being happy for his friend, started to lecture him on the Osu caste system. He warned his friend that the Diala in the community would think he was an Osu if he continued to date the girl. This shows how primitive and destructive the system could be.

The young man could not comprehend the implications of the culture at first, but he pressed on with stories associated with the system and showed him the Osu section of the community. When the story was all over, it was like waking up from a dream after a terrible headache had cleared and he pulled himself together. Since this young man did not want to limit his chances of dating other beautiful girls in the community, he caved in to social pressure. It did not take long for the girl to know that her friend had discovered social status because the young man had started 'to act funny' and eventually abandoned the beautiful young girl.

This and similar stories show how primitive and destructive the system could be. A *NewsWatch*[6] investigative report on Oruku community in Nkanu East Local Government Area of Enugu State tells another sad story. As mentioned earlier, the Umuode people (the Osu descendants) in the Oruku community were ostracized, and at a point, driven away from their community by the two other villages (Umuchiani and Onuogowo) that make up Oruku town.

In Akwa-Ekiti in Anambra State, the Osu and the Diala (like in many other communities) live in different parts of the community.[7] Any person from the designated Osu area is automatically a pariah, irrespective of ones beauty, education or wealth. An Osu is treated with contempt like the lowest species of mankind. In a society such as Nigeria where there are no enforceable laws to protect the people's human rights, an Osu is often exposed to public ridicule. Even if the Osu is not being ridiculed in public they carry with them the dehumanizing Osu caste stigma. The crusade for human rights and fundamental freedom has been going on for centuries.[8] As Thomas Jefferson[9] asserts:

> We hold these truths to be self-evident, that all men are created equal, that they are endowed by their Creator with certain inalienable Rights, that among these are Life, Liberty and the pursuit of Happiness....

Since 1948 many International Human Rights Treaties have been negotiated. These include the International Covenant on Civil and Political Rights (1966) and the International Convention on the Elimination of All Forms of Racial Discrimination (1965). The Universal Declaration of Human Rights that the UN Commission on Human Rights prepared (Chaired by Eleanor Roosevelt and endorsed by the United Nations General Assembly on December 10, 1948) stands as the cornerstone document for human rights. Today Dec10 is widely commemorated as Human Rights Day![10]

There are also regional agreements on human rights. The African Charter of Human and People's Rights signed in 1981, but put in force in 1986, is said to be the weakest of the regional human rights efforts.[11] Most of the provisions are not enforced because of weak regulatory institutions in Africa. As the Universal Declaration of Human Rights says, nobody should be denied human and civil rights based on race, color, sex, language, religion, political or other opinions, national and social origin (descent) or birth.

2). Civil Rights Implications

One of the objectives of this book is highlighting inequality and unfair human relationships. A person should enjoy his or her civil rights (see the definition on chapter one) without hindrance. Freedom to do or worship evil is a vice, as it is the matter with the Osu caste system. Democracy "demands that the human personality in its course of development should be allowed to proceed without artificial forces or barricade, as long as the activity does not violate the safety and reasonable rights of others."[12]

The social development of a nation (or a community) must include justice, fairness, and equal treatment for everyone. With this the society may achieve a desirable "unity in diversity."[13]Thus civilized societies that are by "affirmation democratic" should "provide and protect ..." the civil rights of its citizens.[14]And any person who violates a person's civil rights should be given due consequences without fear, or favor, ill will or affection.

People should do what is right. Socrates says, "He who knows what good is will do good." And only the person who does what is right can be a "virtuous" person. But one wonders why people are not listening. The Osu 'inhumanity' is bad, but it is still around. The society should condemn and discard it! We can only fool the rest of the world briefly by pretending that we do not know that the system is wrong. But this system is long over due!

3). Political Implications

The end of politics as Aristotle notes is for the "Good of man and for building well-organized society." But why have the political leaders not been able to eradicate the discriminatory Osu system?

The system is politically unpalatable. Some people would argue that the present Igbo generation does not have the authority to destroy what they inherited from their forefathers. And this group would regard as insane any person who suggests the jettisoning of the system. As mentioned earlier, some would think any person who is fighting against the system must be an Osu. One does not have to be an Osu to speak against injustice and discrimination.

Like ethnicity, the system could influence a person's voting behavior. In some communities the diehard would not give political support to an "Osu" for political office to represent the community, even if that person is a better-qualified politician than the "Diala". This group could vote against any person who suggests the jettisoning of the system.

This type of behavior is common at the local level where most of the supporters of the system live. This type of behavior prevents the rejected person from contributing to the development of their community. Those appointed to political offices could lose their positions should they protest any ill treatment against the Osu. As noted earlier, Morris Ede (a former Commissioner for special duties in Enugu State-an Umuode indigene) protested the manner in which the Governor of Enugu State handled the Osu crisis in Oruku community. Morris Ede was let go when the Governor reshuffled his cabinet.[15]

Community development projects could be abandoned because a project is located in an Osu community. For instance, Ifakala community in Mbaitolu Local Government Area (Imo State) had no good source of water supply and the nearest stream in the area is about eight kilometers away. The State under the leadership of late Governor Sam Mbakwe in the 1980's decided to help the community with a pipe-borne water scheme. But a few days before the taps would begin to run rumors began to circulate that the village that the project was located in an "Osu" neighborhood. For them the location of the project in the rejected community made the 'water unfit for human consumption.' Consequently, the project was abounded.[16] Political and cultural pressure make it difficult for individuals (who in private would condemn the system) to fall-short of the forensic condemnation of the primitive practice. And any person who resists the pressure and associates with the Osu is greeted with derision, social persecution, and ostracism.

The Osu system is a repressive culture and, therefore, should be eradicated. In spite of the increase in the level of education very little changes, if any, have occurred in the area of the ancient system. Peace and justice is the prime element in human relationship. When justice is violated a society suffers; there will be no harmony, and the society will not progress.

Conclusion

Individually and collectively, all Igbos are culpable, for not taking necessary steps to eradicate the system. The campaign must begin with you! As Mahatma Gandhi (1869-1948) notes "The only devils in the world are those running around in our own hearts. That is where the battle should be fought." Thus, it is morally wrong to subject a part of a community to perpetual misery. You are judged by your actions! Let this ancient belief system die!

Chapter 6
Notes and References

1. Jostein Gaarder: Sophie's World-A Novel about the History of Philosophy (New York: Berkeley Books, March 1996), p.132

2. Amartya Sen: Development As Freedom. Random House, 1999

3.The Eastern Regional government of Nigeria (1956): 'The Law promulgated to outlaw the Osu system by the then Eastern Regional government of Nigeria in 1956 was not effective.'

4. Nnamdi Azikiwe: "Essentials for Nigerian Survival" (Foreign Affairs—An American Quarterly Review), April 1965, vol. 43, No. 3, p.455

5. The Punch: (See article by Kupoluyi) on how the Osu culture prevented a young man from dating a lady who caught his attention in a town in Imo State, Nigeria. *The Punch*: January 10, 1996

6. Tobs Agbaegbu: "Moves to stop slavery in Igboland;" NewsWatch, Vol. 31, No. 1, 12 Jan 2000); and "Slavery in Igboland" (NewsWatch, 12 Jan 2000)

7. Victor E. Dike: 'The Osu Caste System in Igboland: Discrimination Based on Descent;' (CERD) Sixty-first session, Geneva (8-9 August 2002)

8. The Encyclopedia Americana: International Edition:—Grolier—Vol.6, 1999 pp.768-776 (Also vol.14, 1999, pp.552c-552h). Also see The Lectric Law Library—Lexicon on Rights: (www.192.41.4.29/def2/q167.htm)

9. Thomas Jefferson: (USHistor.org): "IN CONGRESS, JULY 4, 1776: The unanimous Declaration of the thirteen United States of America;" also See: www.ushistory.org/declaration/document/index.htm (accessed April 13, 2006).

10. The Encyclopedia Americana: International Edition:—Grolier—Vol.6, 1999 pp.768-776 (Also vol.14, 1999, pp.552c-552h). Also see *The Universal Declaration of Human Rights* (Chaired by Eleanor Roosevelt in 1948), which the UN Commission on Human Rights prepared and which the UN General Assembly endorsed on Dec. 10, 1948.

11. Ibid.

12. Ibid.

13. Gordon W. Allport: The Nature of Prejudice (25th Ed.) (Addison-Wesley Pub. 1979)

14. T.V. Smith and Edward C. Lindeman: The Democratic Way of Life. N.Y: Mentor Books, 1985

15. Tobs Agbaegbu: "Moves to stop slavery in Igboland" (NewsWatch, Vol. 31, No. 1, 12 Jan 2000); and "Slavery in Igboland;" NewsWatch, 12 Jan 2000

16. Tobs Agbaegbu: Ibid.

17. *Nigerian Tribune* (January 14, 2007); Jude Ossai "Osu Caste in Igboland"

7

The Osu Caste Discrimination and Community Development

This short chapter deals with the impacts of the Osu system on community development. Societies are faced with many problems human beings do not have answers to. Any problem created by human beings has a solution, and should tirelessly pursue the quest for solutions to human problems. Without this social development would be negatively affected.

Human Behavior and Community Discord

It has been emphasized that the Osu system has caused lots of community conflicts and discords in Igboland. In 1995, the Oruku community drove the people of Umuode out of their land and many lives and properties were destroyed.[1,2] There were communal clashes, also, in the clans of Umuawuka and Emii in Owerri LGA, Imo State.[3,4] Again, a water project in Ifakala Community in the 1980s was abandoned because it was 'located on Osu land.'[5] For the Diala the location of the project in the supposed Osu community makes the water unfit for drinking; this is ridiculous!

In late 1980s in Umuaka community (Imo State) some skirmishes occurred between the Diala and the Osu section of the community.[6,7,8] And around Sept-Oct 2003, there was a riot in the "Osu" section of the community because of a misunderstanding among the people over a name-change. A group of people in Amafor believed that the old name, which identifies them as Osu was bringing them ill-luck and bad image and, therefore, wanted the village to adopt a new name and riots ensued when they could not agree on a name. A couple of people sustained injuries and local shops were looted; *Obinwanne* is its new name.

The system has caused untold hardship and communal clashes in the clans of Umuawuka and Emii in Owerri LGA, Imo State.[9,10]As noted earlier, in Ifakala Community in the 1980s a water project was abandoned because the Diala complained that the project was 'located on "Osu" land.'[11] The Osu caste system is very costly to ignore.

Social Psychological Cost of the Osu caste Discrimination

This section deals with the social psychological impact of discrimination and oppression. Experts have noted that those who perpetrate prejudice and discrimination against others do not wish them well. Discrimination has been shown to adversely affect the health of "marginalized" groups. Discrimination is associated with mental health and physical stress symptoms; it also affects people's self-esteem. In a study "Blacks" who experience discrimination could develop social, psychological, and physiological problems. Some health-related problems include 'high blood pressure, heart attacks, strokes, kidney failure and depression.'[12]

Discrimination hinders the social mobility of those being discriminated against; it causes psychological and health problems. Although no work has been done in this area, the Osu is expected to have similar problems faced by others. The social costs of discrimination are staggering, including isolation; barriers to relationships; ostracism from other group; violence and unrest; insecurity and loss of resources and knowledge to foster social well being. And some of the psychological costs include mental health problems.[13]

The Osu Caste Discrimination: Social Dimension and Community Development

Community development has broad and varied definitions. It is the practices and academic disciplines of civic leaders, activists, involved citizens and professionals to improve various aspects of local communities.[14] Community development is the process of working with local communities and supporting them to identify their needs, develop their skills and confidence and decide upon appropriate action. To participate effectively in community development one must be free from discrimination and to control factors that affects their social well being.

How would one participate in community development projects if the person oppressed and stigmatized by the system? The welfare of every individual in a community matter and every society must work harder to ensure it. The culture of a people is an important variable in their social progress. When the people in a community are segregated and freedom of association is restricted, social development is obviously impacted. Thus any culture that is discriminatory is antithetical to the 'principle of globalization' and human progress.

Fairness, equity and justice demand that the communities practicing the system should work harder to bridge their "Osu divide." An Igbo adage says, 'He who thinks that the human flesh would make delicious meat should pinch his or her skin to see how painful it feels.' The Osu caste discrimination remains a challenge to Igbo culture and civilization. Those discriminating against their fellow human beings are ignorant of the implications on community development. The 1995 incident in the Oruku community where the people of Umuode were driven out of their land is a good example of the dangers of practice.[15]The system encourages segregation, violates people's rights and negatively impacts their development.

Some projects have been abandoned because of the issue. For instance, a pipe borne water project proposed in Ifakala Community in the 1980s because the Diala community complained that the project was 'located on Osu land.'[16]Without peace and stability a community cannot implement effective development projects; and this would lead to rising poverty, crime and, misery.

Conclusion

Given the above analysis the Osu system appears to have adversely impacted community development in Igboland. The culture of the people is their strength and weakness. The system is a pimple in the face of the Igbo nation. Fairness, equity, and justice dictate that people should intensify their efforts in speaking out against the system that oppresses the powerless and voiceless and to discard the obnoxious and ancient system. Also, the NGOs should seek financial assistance from the United Nations (and other international bodies) to form a stronger solidarity with groups that assist individuals whose "basic human rights are jeopardized or completely denied."[17]This will improve the image of the society and the social, psychological and economic conditions of the oppressed.

Chapter 7
Notes and References

1. Tobs Agbaegbu: "Moves to Stop Slavery in Igboland;" NewsWatch, 12 Jan 2000

2. Civil Resource Development and Documentation Center: "Gross Violation of Human Rights: A Call On Nigeria Human Rights Community to Take Action;" Enugu State, Nigeria, 1999

3. Daily Sunray: "Scars of Communal Clash Still Haunt Emii." Port Harcourt: May 7, 1993

4. Sebastian Mbaonu Obi: How to Solve the Osu Problem. Owerri, Nigeria: Agape Edu. Resources, 1994

6. Ely Obasi, et al.: "The God's are to Blame;" Newswatch, Sept.18, 1989

7. Jude O. Ezeala: See Lecture at Nekede Polytechnic (Jan 18, 1992); and Jude O. Ezeala: Can the Igboman be a Christian in View of the Osu Caste System? Orlu, Nigeria: B. I. Nnaji & Sons, 1991

8. Victor E. Dike: "The Caste System in Nigeria, Democratization and Culture: Socio-political and Civil Rights Implications." Africa Economic Analysis—www.afbis.com, June 13, 1999

9. Victor E. Dike: "Community Development and the Osu Caste Discrimination"-www.gamji.com/NEWS3257.htm, January 2004

10. Sebastian Mbaonu Obi: How to Solve the Osu Problem. Owerri, Nigeria: Agape Educational Resources, 1994; and Isaiah Ilo: "Christians Vs Osu Taboo: The Ragging Battle in Eastern Nigeria;" Today's Challenge, 2, 1992

11. Ely Obasi, et al.: "The God's are to Blame;" Newswatch, Sept.18, 1989

12. Jet: "Why discrimination is detrimental to the health of blacks—study of high blood pressure finds correlation to race discrimination;" Jet, November 25, 1996. Johnson Publishing Co.

13. The University of Vermont: Discrimination: Race & Culture—on the costs of discrimination-www.uvm.edu/culture/site: accessed June 29, 2004; also see *Richard Rorty:* (ed.) "Human Rights, Rationality and Sentimentality;" in The Politics of Human Rights. London: The Belgrade Circle, 1999

14. Community Development: en.wikipedia.org/wiki/Community_ development; accessed April 10, 2006

15. Tobs Agbaegbu: "Moves to Stop Slavery in Igboland;" NewsWatch, 12 Jan 2000

16. Ely Obasi, et al.: "The God's are to Blame;" Newswatch, Sept.18, 1989

17. Obrad Savic: (ed.) "Introduction: The Global and the Local in Human Rights;" in The Politics of Human Rights. London: Veros-The Belgrade Circle, 1999

8

Breaking Down the Osu Caste Barriers: A New Agenda for Change

We have come a long way in laying the theoretical foundation and thinking about the ethical dimensions of Osu caste discrimination. But it is not good enough to discuss the issue without finding a solution to the problem. This chapter, thus, gives us an opportunity as it recommends a New Agenda for change! As Albert Einstein notes "The significant problems we face [today] cannot be solved at the same level of thinking we were at when we created them."

1. Education

Sporadic efforts to eliminate the problem have not been fruitful because only changing the culture and education of the people and "their psychological make-up" (this is long process) can eliminate the sources of the problem. Some of the new approaches to the problem include legislative and law enforcement, grass-roots education and religious intervention, media campaigns, individual contact and Dialogue, and personal therapy.

One of the steps towards solving the Osu caste discrimination is education. The main purpose of education is to remedy ignorance. Education involves transformation of the citizenry and making them aware of their rights and duties in the society. Also proper education could enable the people to understand and recognize when their rights and those of the others are being violated.

Without some positive changes in the mentality (or mindset) of the supporters of the system, no "sermon on the mount" or institutional sledgehammer would resolve this long-standing social dilemma. The Igbo society is capable of moving away from "the primitive aspect" of its good cultural heritage; and that is a challenge facing everyone. As John F. Kennedy notes, "One man can make a difference, but every man should try."

The village remains the bastion of strong belief regarding the system and the campaign should, therefore, start there. In other words, they should be the main targets of this enlightenment campaign, which if properly done, would reduce, if not eradicate, the Osu prejudice and discrimination in the society. And through human rights education the people "will recognize the legitimacy, beauty and full potential of every human being and every human group."[1] Thus, if you educate the people, you create awareness, reduce ignorance, and increase social interaction. The Osu caste discrimination has its roots in the beliefs widely shared among the people in the past. But the old beliefs have lingered; there is need for consistent and continuous campaign to effect changes.

The grassroots education should be undertaken in local dialects (as the main supporters of the system are not well educated). Human Rights organizations and policymakers should play role in the civic education. And parents and guardians should instruct their children not to engage in any discriminatory practices. They should teach them by good examples, because learning to respect other people's rights is an important step toward changing the peoples' mindset.

The schools have important roles to play. Thus the society should provide them with the resources to instruct and educate the public, because they should not be expected to perform miracles without the necessary resources. The educated elite has important role to play too; they could serve as good role models to the youths by leading the campaign against the Osu system. An educated person is "somebody who has learned how to learn, and who continues learning, especially by formal education throughout his or her lifetime."[2]

Teachers should be properly trained and motivated to play a leading role and school curricula should be modified to teach respect for human rights and to obey the laws of the land. Respect for human rights begin from the institutions (the home, school, church, etc) individual is exposed to during the person's formative years. Planting the right ideas in the minds of the youths would help to destroy the stereotypes that surround the Osu and to develop friendly attitudes towards the "marginalized and oppressed" group. In general, the more educated the society is, the easier and quicker it could find solutions to its problems.

The government (federal, state and local) should empower the people, so as to enhance their ability to challenge the oppressive ancient system. The citizens should learn to always do the right thing. As Thomas Aquinas succinctly notes "We see life in terms of ought and ought not" and to "do good and avoid evil."[3]

With appropriate laws of the land and good court systems, the people could seek redress in court if their rights are violated.

2. Legislation

Tackling the Osu caste discrimination in Igboland should involve enacting appropriate and enforceable laws against the system. This is because effective regulatory structures are needed to implement any law. In the mid-50s, the then Eastern Nigerian Colonial Legislative Council under the leadership of the late Owelle of Onitsha, Nnamdi Azikiwe, passed a legislation that outlawed the Osu caste practice. The law made it a criminal offense to discriminate against anyone on the basis of the system. But the law, like other laws in Nigeria, was rendered impotent, as it was not enforced.[4,5] That was in the 1950's; although Nigeria faces many problems today, there are more educated citizens today than in the 1950s. That the law was not enforced does not mean that better legislated and enforceable laws would not be effective in this 21st century.

The States from the former Eastern Region should re-visit the law (amend it). And the National Assembly should pass laws that would outlaw any form of discrimination in Nigeria and include penalties, such as payment of serious fine, a jail term, etc. Strict enforceable penalties could deter violators of the law. The democratization process in the society would not be complete without adequate provisions to tackle rampant human and civil rights violations in the country.

The Osu caste problem should be faced proactively because passive approach would not solve the problem. Without good policies no society would progress. Some people would argue that not every social problem could be settled through legislation. And that Biblical injunction has not been able to provide everlasting love between neighbors. Any legislation demanding people to love one another may not be effective without first changing their mind-set.

Enforceable laws could tackle the Osu palaver because the de-segregation of schools in the United States involved a "long array of constitutional decisions."[6] Appropriate legal prods and the mass media are necessary and the time is now!

3. The Mass Media

The mass media has critical role to play in the campaign to dismantle the Osu caste barrier. It should do this by disseminating appropriate information to the public, educating them of their rights and how to respect the rights of others. In other words, the mass media should educate both victims and the oppressors (the Osu and the Diala) of their rights and what they should do if their rights are violated. Without this the grassroots campaign against the system may not be fruitful. It is the responsibility of the mass media to report cases of human rights and civil rights abuses to the appropriate authorities for necessary actions. This will help to promote and protect the civil and human rights of the citizenry. The role of religion in every society is also important.

4. Religion and Tolerance

Religion is important to many people. A truly religious faithful is a good individual. Religious teaching could influence people's behavior (can change the mentality of the people and the way they perceive the system) and thus help to dismantle the Osu barrier. But if individuals seek God's blessing in their own undertaking why would they wish others evil? If you hate and discriminate against any person, you are not wishing that person well!

Religious organizations should redouble their efforts in educating their members on the need for tolerance. Common sense (everyone has it, but not everyone uses it) dictates that everyone needs love! The society should always use it conscience (ability to differentiate right and wrong—but this varies from one person to another). Some people use their bad conscience instead of good conscience; people have different 'philosophy of life' (affected by upbringing, environment and values). It requires personal courage and individual intelligence to differentiate right from wrong and to free oneself 'from the prevailing views' of the time.[7]

Christians, Muslims, Buddhists, Osu, and Diala should respect one another and to live in harmony. The highly respected religious leaders: Priests, Pastors, Imams, etc. could effect some meaningful changes in the society, if they should work in schools, foster homes, and other institutions where the youths congregate. They should take up the challenge of educating the people against the Osu caste discrimination. While the ignorance of the past could be pardoned or overlooked but the greatest regret is that some of the so-called Igbo Christians are stilling looking down on their "Osu" kinsmen. The task of restoring the dignity of the "Osu" people rests squarely on the shoulders of Igbo Christians. Thus religious leaders (and traditional rulers) should call their people to order when they go astray and not to be hypocritical. As Bishop Alexander Ezeugo Ekewuba (General Overseer of Over-comers Christian Church in Owerri) asked, "How many pastors will allow their children to marry an Osu person?"[8]

The Ohanaeze Ndigbo (a socio-cultural Pan-Igbo group) noted during its presentation at the Justice Oputa human rights panel that marginalization is "purposeful denial of rights of some members of a given unit by some other members of the group who control the power of allocation of resources. The Ohanaeze Ndigbo perceives 'marginalization' of Ndigbo as:

> The denial of right to life and right to means of livelihood, right to Human dignity, right to freedom of movement, right to freedom from discrimination, right to acquire and own immovable property anywhere in Nigeria, and other rights enshrined in the constitution.[9]

This is hypocritical because the Diala in the group knows that they are also marginalizing the Osu. The churches and Ohanaeze Ndigbo should understand the desperation and uncertainty that marks the lives of this group and begin to teach the youths that the Osu discrimination (and other forms) is wrong.

5. Contact and Dialogue

Social re-education can make a lot of difference as that could translate into greater social contact and dialogue. As noted earlier, there are some stereotypes associated to the Osu that are because of lack of contact with the group. Social contacts are good steps to erasing the stereotypes. Social programs that encourage contacts are necessary to eradicate the prevailing stereotypes.

Contacts and acquaintances make for friendliness. When people dismantle the social barriers to relationship and find out that they have everything in common, discrimination would disappear. Communication could help to break up the Osu barriers. Ignorance is part of the obstacles to dismantle the barriers. Friendly dialogue could help in understanding one another better. As Kweisi Mfume[10] notes

> When you understand more, you are more sensitive; when you are more sensitive, you are more compassionate. When you are more compassionate, you are more prepared to see the other side of the issue.

However, the victims of the caste system should be in the forefront in the struggle to eradicate the Osu caste discrimination and organize themselves effectively to fight the battle for emancipation. Many of them are ashamed to publicly admit their "Osu" status; they should push the issue to the front line of community, national and international discourse.

6. Individual Therapy

Those who have problems respecting the rights of others should consider seeking some therapy. However, individual therapy (or group) is said to be foreign in

Africa, because they do not want strangers to know their personal problems. In spite of this, therapy could help to correct false beliefs regarding the Osu system.[11]

The governments (federal, state, and local) and Non-governmental organizations should set up counseling centers where those who could not afford private therapy should go for some mental re-adjustment on how to respect other people's human and civil rights. Counseling could help to change the mentality and attitude of the gullible "ignorant" and "illiterate" population who are propagating the system. Nobody wants to be sad and angry and as Anwar El-Sadat notes "There is [or should be] no happiness for people at the expense of others."

7. The Court and the Law Enforcement

The police and the court should protect the people from abuse. But the Nigerian police and the judicial system, like every other part of the society, is corrupt. Corrupt judges are on the bench; thereby perverting justice.[12] Justice Akanbi notes Nigerians have not done enough to emancipate the society from the civil burdens of corruption. God will not change the precarious——situations [in Nigeria] until we are ready to change our perception of life.[13]

There are many laws in Nigeria, but a law is useful only when it is implemented. The police are either too corrupt to perform their duties or the judges who handle the case are corrupt and thus pervert justice. A special court and police unit should be created to handle discrimination cases. They should be instructed not to sit on any case because justice delayed is justice denied. The rule should be, 'do unto others as you would have them do unto you.'

8. Conversion of Osu to Diala

One of the solutions to the Osu caste discrimination would be the provision of opportunity for the so-called "Osu" to be converted to Diala through special ceremonies as the case in India where the low-caste Hindus (Dalits) have the opportunity to adopt new faith and be converted to Buddhism and Christianity. By converting the Dalits (untouchables) to Buddhism and Christianity they could escape the prejudice and discrimination the group normally face. However, several states governed by the Hindu nationalist party (the BJP), have introduced laws to make the conversions more difficult. The laws are purely political as conversions away from Hinduism erode the BJP's bedrock support.[14]

9. Can Autonomous Community Status Help?

The Osu system is unique and common sense demands that a variety of measures should be adopted to tackle it. The Osu victims should 'grab the bull on the horn' and set up self-help organizations to fight for equal treatment under the law. They should do whatever it takes to gain freedom! As Margaret Thatcher says "You may have to fight a battle more than once to win it." And as Mahatma Gandhi says, "You must be the change you wish to see in the world."

Many communities are now on the quest for autonomous status. With this the oppressed groups could re-define themselves and determine their fate and control their destiny. The "Osu" group would be better to work for autonomous status. Their destiny is in their hand! As the lyric of Bob Marley and the Wailers implores,' Get up, stand up, and fight for your rights.... Get up, stand up, and don't give up the fight....' Living in the midst of the "Diala" is tantamount to drawing a definite circle or building a brick wall around them for life. Miracles do not happen any more! Human beings ('mortals') should not 'sit just idly by and wait for the gods [or God] to intervene' while they perish.[15]

These are not by any means exhaustive because this project is a small effort at tackling the mammoth social problem. Many people are still hanging on the beliefs of the primitive era. One of the reasons true democracy has for long eluded Nigeria has been the inability of the society to pull out of the mire of yesterdays thinking. Tyrants are worshipped like the gods, while they trample on the rights of others. Where there is no justice there is no happiness, social cohesion, and progress.

Conclusion

Injustice has been perpetrated in other societies, like the United States and South Africa. Some people are now advocating that the US should pay restitution and render apology for the violation of the civil rights of the "Blacks" in the 1960s. As Randall Robinson notes "White" race owes Africans 'moral debt' for their humiliation and exploitation.[16] In the same token the Igbo community should dismantle the Osu caste system, render an unreserved apology, and pay restitution to the victims. The Igbo is a hardworking and peace-loving group, but the Osu Caste System and its discriminatory tendencies, is a pimple on the face of the Igbo culture and her civilization.

Chapter 8
Notes and References

1. **The National Center for Human Rights Education** (NCHRE): www.nchre.org (accessed April 13, 2006)

2. **Peter F. Drucker:** "The Age of Social Transformation;" The Atlantic Monthly, November 1994, Vol. 274, No. 5; pp.53-80

3. **Quentin L. Quade:** "Ethics in a Pluralistic Society: the Need for School Choice." In Virgil C. Blum, Center for Parental Freedom in Education, April 22, 1998

4. **National Archive** (Enugu): Legislation against Osu Cult (1935-1955), OP1322, ONDIST 12.1.873); www.2hu-berlin.de/orient/nae/gridx.htm#0 (accessed Dec 2005)

5. **Okenwa Nwosu:** (June 19, 1999) "Osu Caste System: A Cultural Albatross for the Igbo Society;" accessed October 2006—www.nigeriaworld.com.

6. **Gordon W. Allport:** The Nature of Prejudice (25th ed.). Addison-Wesley Pub. 1979

7. **Jostein Gaarder:** Sophie's World-A Novel about the History of Philosophy. New York: Berkeley Books, March 1996, pp.124-125

8. **Daily Sun** (Nov 2, 2004). **"Igbos will never be president unless they stop serving idols"**

9. **Emmanuel Onwubiko:** "Eight arraigned at Anti-graft Panel;" Guardian: Monday, December 18, 2000.

10. **Kweisi Mfume:** (see Modern Maturity Magazine): Interview with Claudia Dreifus, March-April 2000, pp.51-63

11. See "Group Therapy or Individual Therapy" (accessed April 11, 2006) http://web4health.info/en/answers/therapy-group-vs-individual.htm

12. **Babafemi Ojudu and Alex Kabba:** "The Judges Are Liars;" Tempo Newspaper—volume 2, No. 4, January 27, 1994, pp.3-5

13. Emmanuel Onwubiko: "Eight arraigned at Anti-graft Panel;" Guardian: Monday, December 18, 2000.

14. BBC News: "Low-caste Hindus adopt new faith," Saturday, Oct 14, 2006.

15. Jostein Gaarder: Sophie's World-A Novel about the History of Philosophy New York: Berkeley Books, March 1996, pp.124-125

16. Randall Robinson: (2000) Debt: What America Owes To Blacks; A Plume Book

9

Public Reaction to the Osu Absurdity

"Courage is what it takes to stand up and speak; courage is also what it takes to sit down and listen." Winston Churchill

The Osu palaver often sparks off interesting debates whenever it is mentioned, including on the Internet. One of such discussions took place on the Igbo-forum (a yahoo group) recently, which this author collated. The discussions are published here for a wider audience, after the contributors were collectively informed through the group's e-mail on Monday, July 18, 2005. The selected discussions are from Okenwa Nwosu, Chris Aniedobe, Obi Nwakamma, Oliver Mbamara, Nwa-Mazi Eze ABC Udogwu, and Anuri Nnodum.

1) Obi Nwakamma (Igbo_forum@yahoo.com, July 10, 2005)

Unfortunately, because we have been (mis) educated in the English language, we have become very susceptible to terminological errors in our current conception of the Igbo world. The writer of "The Osu in Igbo land" says the meaning of "Osu" in Igbo is slave; a bit like the Ohu or even the Ume; these definitions could be disputed. Ohu, for instance, is not a slave; he or she is an indentured servant. Strictly speaking, slavery does not exist in the Igbo world, because there is nothing final to that relationship.

The Ohu can work themselves out of their indenture. In many instances, the Ohu may even become fully adopted into the family to which it is indentured, after a particular ritual to ala, which confers a ritual link—amadi—to the individual, who is then accorded all the rights of the Diala. But speaking specifically about the Osu—there were two phases: in the first phase, the "Osu" was part of the complex priestly system to the Igbo ritual world. The Igbo world was a highly spiritual system in which the four elements in nature were recreated and symbolized: Ala (Earth) Ogwugwu/Ime muru ochie/Idemili (water) Agwu (wind) Anyanwu (Fire).

The Igbo instituted the rites of Amadi-Oha as a reminder against the use of force or the domestication of energy for deployment in war. It was part of the covenant with Chukwu, and it was also the beginning of the pacific idea in Odi-nala, that the Igbo would never use such instruments of massive force. The serpent of fire—the sign of Ogwugwu—is said to guard Amadi-oha from returning with his fiery energy to earth. It is also said that whoever commits the high abomination on earth suffers the fate Amadi-Oha exemplifies, which is what gave rise to the myth that Amadi-Oha is the earth's messenger in the event of alu ("aru" or evil).

The Igbo had [and still have] Shrines. Every community had the shrine of Ala, Ogwugwu, Agwu or Amadi-oha (which gradually replaced "Ihu-Anyanwu"). The Priests of these Shrines were called Ezeala, EzeOgwuwgwu, Eze Amadioha or EzeAgwu (ndi "isi mmuo".) They had specific rituals and specific seasons connected with the movement of the nature or with celebrations, festivals and according to the covenants of each clan.

There were in the Igbo world those who dedicate themselves (or were dedicated to the service of these shrines). And they were called Osu. It does not quite mean "slave." The closest example of the function of the Osu in the traditional Igbo world is what monks do in Catholic Church or the in Buddhist temples. They chose a life of complete surrender to the deities. Traditionally, they were regarded highly. In fact, the names, Osuji, Osuagwu, Osuala, Nwosu, etc did not confer extraordinary negation. To this day, many Igbo bear these names, and they are not "Osu" in the Osu caste notion of the word.

The second phase of the system, when it became endowed with increasing negative connotations was at the height of the slave raids in the Igbo world in the 19th century. The Osu had begun to be seen as largely a parasitic institution. They were immune from too many things. They had the best portion of the land, they did not work (and they became subjects of both envy and derision in a most difficult era in the Igbo world), which demanded hard work and enterprise for survival. At the height of the slave raids, some very vulnerable people chose to dedicate themselves to the service of deities, or were dedicated by their families to the altar, so that they would [not be sold into slavery and therefore] became literally "untouchable." In time, these groups metamorphosed into isolation from the rest of the community and became subjects of fear, envy and disdain.

This was the state of affairs until missionaries entered the Igbo world late in the 19th century. The first group of people to be evangelized was the Osu. The missionaries, of course, saw in their ritual isolation, a condition akin to the Indian caste system, and propagated the dubious picture of a ritually isolate, ritually ex-communicated caste community, and gave the Osu the bad name that continues today in Igboland.

Traditionally, there was no hereditary Osu. It was, in fact, a privileged institution, until its desecration, both by evolving political and economic reality and by the transformations in the ritual meaning given to it by Christianity. Osu means someone totally dedicated or enslaved to a particular cause. Whatever that cause was is ancient history but what it says to me is that anyone who looks down on a fellow Igbo man because their forbears were once enslaved to a particular cause, is not one, two, but three times a fool. (Obi Nwakamma (Igbo_forum@yahoo.com), July 10, 2005.)

2) Chris Aniedobe—E-mail (July 11, 2005)

UmuIbe:

I do not have the scholarship to get into any credible historical synthesis of the Osu institution in Ani Igbo, but I have the philosophical and analytical tools to make reasoned, if unstudied inquiries thereto and I intend to do that in response to Okenwa's poser. First some background information.

As I said before Igbo names and Igbo language bear a scent that trails authentic Igbo history. Osu as an Igbo word has been taken classically to mean one enslaved to a deity or one dedicated to a deity. Fair enough. But Osu as a prefix, such as OsuUka, OsuOfia, OsuNta, OsuUgbo etc is also used in Igbo language to mean being totally dedicated to a cause. Who is to say that Nwosu does not mean NwosuOfia or Nwosunta or NwosuUgbo etc? Osu as an Igbo word is not necessarily related to the deity usage of that word. As to the deity usage of Osu as in Osuagwu or OsuOgwugwu or Osuani and its non-deity usage such as OsuOfia or OsuNta, I do not have sufficient scholarship to tell you the one that came first. Our born again Christians today would be called Osu Christi in relation to their enslavement to the word of Christ. It is a badge to be won with honor and so as the Osu of any particular deity was not always a tag that invited scorn and derision.

There is no Igbo community that I am aware of that Osu is associated with a stigma. Although Nwankama asserts that being Osu was not a stigma, there is no empirical evidence of that assertion in contemporary Igbo society. Going back to the name thing as a source of empirical deductions, it makes sense, and I can say it without contradiction, that people who bear the name Osu in (such as Nwosu, Osuji, Osuagwu) are not necessarily related to the Osu institution. Even if there were, such names would not be won with pride if it would subject the person to scorn and derision. It means that whatever ties those names have with the institution of Osu is an immensely positive tie.

The Igbos bears Osu in their name with pride. And I feel safe, in conclusion, to say that if those names represent ties in one way or the other with the Osu institution, it is at least some evidence that being an Osu was not always a stigma. It might have been something that was praise-worthy or inducing great pride in one's heritage. Osu arises by inheritance—a child of Osu remains an Osu. Osu also arises against the will of another.

Secondly, powerful oracles sometimes decree that a family furnish a person in order to atone for a wrong done by that family. Such persons furnished from whatever source become dedicated to those deities and become Osus. Chances too are that those persons must belong to an underprivileged class. Thirdly, and I suspect, a great majority of people become Osus out of their own volition (as a way to commit themselves to the patronage of a particular deity and avoid persecution.) Chances are too that the people likely to fly to the patronage of a deity are social underclassmen. In all these instances, it appears that being an Osu does not commit one to a socially underprivileged status.

Being an Osu, as I understand it, has its privileges and immunities and that institution must be understood from that angle as well. Once an Osu, it is hands off for every one else, including oppressors. Anyone who persecutes such a person runs the risk of drawing heavy reprisals from the deity to whom they belong. Those people become physically and socially sequestered for fear of incurring the wrath of the deities. In that sense, being an Osu conferred a great social benefit. It meant freedom from oppression and it most definitely meant that a slave hunter would not mess with one dedicated to a powerful deity.

I can imagine a situation in Igbo history when Osus walked as free men and women, wearing the garb of their protection with great pride. That is why I believe that being an Osu has not always carried a negative stereotype. Also, the social avoidance, which attends being an Osu, had nothing to do with the social graces of an Osu, it had everything to do with the fear of the society of messing with what or who belonged to deities.

With that said, I now invite my good friend Okenwa, to reflect on how the Chief Priests related to the Osus. The Chief Priest being an agent of the deities, all Osus dedicated to a particular deity become property of the Chief Priest. Their tie to the greater community is through the Chief Priest and the Chief Priest is the absolute ruler of the Osu community of his deity and whatever he decrees is the decree of the deity. As people enslaved or dedicated to the deities, it is well within the province of the Chief Priest to deal with his Osu community as he pleases.

In conclusion, whatever and however one becomes an Osu, in every empirical consideration, such persons become slaves of the Priests of the deities to which they were dedicated. I rest my case. I join other Osu Christi in rejoicing that the Osu institution is thankfully a thing of the past. No book can probably do justice to it. But anybody who disdains an individual because they had ties with an institution which served such a great social function in Igbo land, such as providing refuge for the underprivileged, is ... a fool." (Chris Aniedobe, E-mail July 11, 2005)

3) Okenwa Nwosu—Reply to the Above E-mail

Chris,

You are definitely extending the mangling process far beyond your client that you are determined to defend at all costs. In the process of arguing your position, you find yourself wallowing deeper in the realm of the unreal. How did you arrive at the idea that Osus dedicated to a deity are personal properties of the shrine's high priest? Where have you heard that high priests sleep with the Osus dedicated to the deities they serve? If you really understand the Osu phenomenon, intimate sexual relationship with the Osus would automatically make the high priest an Osu and thus unfit to retain his exalted position.

I wish the Osu phenomenon were a joking matter to millions who are burdened by its stigma. Even for the non-osu, it is a very serious matter to see artificial impediments placed today in lives of people whose only "crime" is that they happen to be born into a lineage of an ancestral Osu. Almost everyone confronted with this dilemma would advocate abrogation of Osu caste system throughout Alaigbo without further delay. But this cannot be successfully done if those who shall oversee this abrogation are ignorant of the ramifications of this six century-old practice. That is why it is still important that all who really care about ending this practice must first make the necessary effort to understand this phenomenon as much as possible.

Chris, you are my very brilliant mentor any day, your disposition on the Osu issue notwithstanding. I know that your power of advocacy can go a long way in helping to unshackle the invisible bondage that has handicapped a sizeable segment of Igbo kith and kin by preventing them from aspiring to achieve their God-given potentials in mainstream Igbo society. No one is a citadel of knowledge on this matter. Even some of the Osus don't have the slightest idea of what the caste system is all about. But they are nonetheless still ensnared by its aura.

We cannot joke ourselves out of this issue, no matter how much we try to trivialize it. If you have the time let's deliberate further on how to rein in this monster in our lifetime for the sake of our Igbo cultural heritage.

4) Oliver Mbamara (Igbo-forum) July 12, 2005

Umuigbo,

Permit me to add my little piece to the interesting issue of "Osu," "Ohu," "Ume," etc as may be called in Ibo-land. We may pretend that these issues are no longer of any significance in Ibo-land, but the truth is that they continue to matter to many of us. So what do we do? We can take up the mantle and correctly tell our history and stories or we can surrender to the machinations of western education and propaganda aimed at portraying many African practices and concepts as being inferior to western ways of life. We have people who have taken their time to research these topics to properly to educate our people of the true nature of things as they use to be before the later days of corrupt interpretations.

If "Osu" is as bad as it has been presented to the present generation, why would many names of people and villages established in the olden days continue to bear the attachment "Osu?" I know, I might be stepping into a sensitive area here because there may be those of us who belief in western religion with such a passion that they may not pause to question certain tenets of the religion, which has condemned the ways of our forefathers. This is not to exonerate our forefathers from their imperfections of life but the truth is that they tried to live life the best way they could. They were not perfect just as the present world is not perfect.

We cannot fairly join the bandwagon to judge our forefathers so harshly. Most great nations of today, including America and Britain, once went through the dark era of their history. Today, they are not being judged by the tenets of those days of strife and tribulation, rather by the glories of their brightest days. Their historians, scholars and writers have embellished their history with fanfare and glory to the extent that today, even those leaders under whom Africans/blacks suffered intense slavery and discrimination are now remembered with praises and glorification.

Let us wake up from blindly degrading ourselves through concepts such as the "Osu Caste." Let us demonstrate the integrity and "independence" of our own minds by refusing to think so callously of our heritage. We should correctly embellish the truth where it has been painted dark. We alone can free ourselves of this shackle.

Our forefathers did not have the benefit of modern day education to document our heritage, but we are fortunate to know how to read and write while some of these elderly ones are still alive. Many of them are willing to share these stories. Oral tradition has sustained the Ibo custom till today, but it is becoming weak in the face of modern day technology and communication.

Let us package the true stories of our heritage in a manner conducive to the modern man. Let us bring our stories down into our own books, films, lectures, festivals, songs, artworks, etc. Let us correctly tell our story. If we fail to do this, then we must not complain, if we find ourselves living in a world where we are judged by misconceptions of those who do not know better. And we must be prepared to live in an atmosphere stigmatized by the interpretation of those who condemn our ways because their concepts of life differ from ours. Best Wishes. Oliver Mbamara (Igbo-forum), July 12, 2005

5) Nwa-Mazi Eze ABC Udogwu (July 12, 2005)

Let us remember that even our domestic dogs deserve pet names, befitting names, and gentle approach, lest they bark and/or bite. I am sorry to say that most Igbo people, paupers as well as dignitaries, are still living in the past glories. Some regaled themselves as infallible "Diala, Igwe, Nze, Ozo." And they cast aspersion on the unfortunate and silent minority whose only crime was their place/status of birth, albeit in the fortresses of those primitive, omnipotent, omniscient but not omnipresent deities and their superhuman cum supernatural agencies. Those bad days are gone!

Today, the Igbo word for priest is "Uko-Chukwu," Osu-Chukwu (Osu-chukwu) [the priest of God] and Osu-Igwe (Osuigwe) [the priest of the heavens]. Others are Osu-Ala (Osuala) [the priest of the land (earth)] and Nwaosu (Nwosu) [son (not child) of the priest], etc. These are befitting Igbo names, which have nothing bigotry about them. Any further attempt to demonize them should be seen as an apish exercise with intent to hurt the concerned. What makes a modern day man/woman is his/her quality of brain [education] and power of knowledge. Our places of birth are gradually fading away into oblivion. Today, the despicable man or woman in Igboland is neither the "Osu nor the Ume, nor the Ohu (Oru) [but the corrupt and dubious elements in the society] (Nwa-Mazi Eze ABC Udogwu, July 12, 2005)

6) Okenwa Nwosu (July 16, 2005)

Otoiheoma,

In Ngo Village, Igboukwu, Anambra State, our people live daily grappling with many contradictions that the Osu and non-Osu divide has inflicted on a community that claims common ancestral heritage. In my administrative village, Akama, the founder had 3 surviving male sons. And as the Igbo custom dictates, inheritance of the parent's obi went to the eldest, Ezeoruizu (Ezeohuizu).

Just before the arrival of colonial rule, Ezeoruizu, who occupied Akama's obi, lost out in a local power play with the nearby village strongman, Ezeumeanolu. When Ezeoruizu was alerted (at the eleventh hour that his nemesis) that Ezeumeanolu had dispatched a raiding party to capture him, he hastily ran to Udo Orti (next door) to his expansive premises and sought shelter from an impending raid and doom. When the raiding party got to Ezeoruizu they could not find him anywhere. But when they learnt that he had run to Udo Orti Shrine for shelter, the raid was called off. However, it spread like wildfire throughout Igboukwu and surrounding communities that Ezeoruizu had elected to become an Osu with his household rather than being humiliated (captured) by a bitter rival. Sadly, the people of Umu Ezeoruizu (kindred) in Akama are today bona fide Osu even though their great grandfather was a titled man who resided at Akama's obi.

Also, Iruowelle (Ihuowelle), the most populous section of Ngo Village, Igboukwu, has a preponderance of Osus for a variety of reasons. The Osu issue should be seen as a great threat to continued survival of Igbo cultural heritage if it is not brought to an end in Alaigbo. Those who appear to benefit from the socio-cultural disorientation of Alaigbo should never be relied upon to lead the way in seeking a lasting solution to Osu problem because they fear the limitless possibilities of a unified Igbo without artificial cleavages that they can exploit.

Any authentic solutions must involve the present custodians of Igbo indigenous religious practice even though their numbers have been declining since the onslaught of superior alien worldview transformed our society. Thus the way forward for the Igbo must include restoration of the authentic indigenous values, which are adjusted to meet the exigencies of the times, but not losing the essence of our culture.

Research informs me that the Osu caste system was not always dominant throughout Alaigbo. The fact that only parts of central Alaigbo practiced the Osu caste system demonstrates the nature of its recent inculcation in the mindset of the Igbos. It was a sort of religious reformation within the original baseline beliefs that underscored Igbo cultural and religious life since antiquity. It may have been valuable in the era in which it played a meaningful role in the religious life of our ancestors. But it time we eliminate this 6 century-old practice before present generation passes it on to the next generation as a mess of inheritance. (Okenwa, July 16, 2005)

7) Anuri Nnodum—Umuakaigbo@aol.com (Tue, 12 Jul 2005)

I am happy that the discussion on this Osu/Ume issue is on now. For those who may not know me, I am the director of the Igbo language and cultural educational program known as the Anuri-umuakaigbo cultural educational program, Inc.

Our Igbo program participants range from youth in kindergarten through college including foreign spouses the Osu issue came up during a folk story lesson centered around a beautiful girl who happened to be an outcast and could not marry the love of her life who happened to be Nwa-Diala. There were serious reactions from some of my older students after this story. One of my female students shared with us the reality in their home now. Her father has said to her and her siblings that they must marry fellow Igbos or at most Nigerians—If not he will disown them.

This girl went further to complain that in her high school she hardly saw an Africans talk less of Nigerians and Igbos and now in college a few of the Igbo guys/Nigerian guys she sported prefer to hang around white girls. Most of her friends are Caribbean and Hispanics. Then she asked me: Dada Anuri, are you saying that if I ever happen to fall in love with an Igbo guy who happens to be an Osu that my father will say no to us getting married? My mouth was suddenly sealed. I was horrified.

Dada Anuri answer me, she went on. Tell me now. I am getting so confused and frustrated. I do not want to miss my chance of being happy in life. I have so many Caribbean and "Akata" (African-Americans) guys who are dying for me. With all this restrictions in my life, I think it is becoming a curse to have been born to an Igbo family. None of my friends ever have to go through any of these. So my brothers and sisters help me to answer these questions (Anuri Nnodum, Tue, 12 Jul 2005).

Conclusion

The contributors in this chapter have done an excellent job in articulating their views on the Osu caste discrimination in Igboland. And the consensus is that the Osu system is a serious challenge for the Igbo Culture and Civilization. Thus, any person reading this book should please share it with another person and pitch in some ideas as to how to resolve the Osu palaver. As Martin Luther King, Jr. says, "Life's most urgent question is what are you doing or have done for others' in need?"

10

Final Thought:
The Osu Caste Discrimination:
To fight it or live with it?

In this final chapter you will have an opportunity to think about yourself and what you would do if you were one of those being discriminated against. The basic question is would you fight or live with the discriminatory Osu caste system?

Changing the People's Mind-set!

It is difficult to effect a social change, especially when it involves changing the culture of a people, without changing the people's ways of thinking. However, positive changes are not impossible to accomplish! As Robert F. Kennedy notes, "Our future may lie beyond our vision, but it is not completely beyond our control." Social change is a "significant alteration of social structures." It is the "patterns of social action and interaction" in a society. Change is "variations or modifications in any aspect of social process, pattern, or form" "Any modification in established patterns of inter-human relationships and standards of conducts."[2]

It appears the Osu problem is a 'hard nut to crack;' but the Igbos should work harder to tackle the problem and build a society worthy to pass on to future generations. Quite often those who are fighting for positive changes are ridiculed and castigated by those who benefit from the status quo. As Niccolo Machiavelli[3] notes:

> … There is neither more delicate matter to take in hand, nor more dangerous to conduct, nor more doubtful in its success, than to set up as a leader in the introduction of changes. For he [who] innovates will have for his enemies all those who are well off under the existing order of things, and [may receive] only lukewarm supporters in those who might be better off under the new.

This lukewarm temper arises partly from the fear of adversaries who have the laws on their side, and partly from the incredulity of mankind, who will never admit the merit of anything new, until they have seen it proved by event. The result, however, is that whenever the enemies of change make an attack, they do so with all zeal of partisans, while others defend themselves so feebly as to endanger both themselves and their cause ...

Change is a constant in contemporary social climates. The people should continue to press for change, especially in the area of the Osu caste discrimination. Individuals, business organizations, and communities should change positively in order to survive in a rapidly changing world. Every organization or community must learn to cope effectively with change, if they are to survive and prosper in the constantly changing world.[4]

Who is benefiting from the primitive system? Nobody does! In the early 1970s, the community of Nnobi, under the leadership of the traditional ruler *Igwe Edmund Ezeokoli II*, announced that the Osu system has been abolished. And recently, Igwe Kenneth Orizu III of Nnewi followed Nnobi, and announced the abolition of the Osu system in Nnewi, Anambra State.[5] Nnokwa, Uli, Enugu-Ezike, and Ifakala have announced on paper that the system has been abolished.[6]The effect of oral pronunciation remains to be seen because it seems difficult for people to change overnight, particularly regarding the issue in discourse! Prejudice and discrimination are destructive. As Kaplan notes, "When prejudice is sufficiently widespread it prevents the formation of [a good] community or destroys whatever sense of [a good] community [that] already exists."[7]

Does the Osu Caste System still Cause Social Disparity?

Those oppressed must understand the danger of being enslaved forever! Does the Osu caste system still cause social disparity in Igboland? Pejorative views of the "Osu" are still depicted in the villages with the arrogant superiority of the "Diala" over the "Osu" shows. Sadly, the cultural practices perpetuating the evil persist; the process of erasing social barriers and distinctions is very slow. Some of the victims have resolved to live with the psychological trauma that alienation begets. But many of them have fled to the cities-'melting pot'-so to say, where the system is less pronounced.

The society should embrace modernity and encourage the love for one another. The problem should be tackled with vigor, because it is not good for the image of the hardworking, resourceful, and intelligent Igbo people. As Okenwa Nwosu[8] passionately notes:

> "I am optimistic that the Igbos are quite capable of doing the right thing for
> their common good, by jettisoning this aspect of their cultural history which
> detracts immensely from the proud heritage of a gifted people."

If the people fail to act, and soon too, posterity would see it in the same fashion as
Shakespeare did, when he said to the immortal Julius Caesar that the "… fault is
not in our star but in ourselves" (Shakespeare 1914). Evil reigns in a society when
good men and women turn a blind eye to evil!

The Igbos should condemn the obnoxious and ancient system because, as
Wole Soyinka notes "The man dies in all who keep silent in the face of tyranny."
Also "justice is the first condition of humanity."[9] It is genuinely the belief of this
author that one day the children of "Osu" and the children of the "Diala" will
join hands and walk together as brothers and sisters! And that should happen
without delay! The 21st Century should mark a positive turning point in solving
the Osu caste discrimination in Igboland.

The Osu caste discrimination is a burden that threatens the culture and unity
of the Igbo people because the cultural and sociological changes occurring in
other sectors of *Igboland* have not impacted the old-age and controversial Osu
issue. The superstitions about the caste system persist in the Igbo community in
spite of increased education and democracy in Nigeria. There is often violence
against those who are working for the eradication of the system.

Throughout this book issue of discrimination, prejudice, and civil and human
rights have been re-visited and useful questions about the Osu discrimination
have been raised. Although rewarding, writing this book has been unsettling,
because it was not certain the answers to the questions were readily available.
Because of the people's cultural mind-set the Osu system is complex, much more
complex than the book tells it, and as such, it would not be exhaustively treated
in this tinny book. Let us hope that the issues raised here will affect some changes
in the people and bring some positive changes to the Osu palaver. This is because
as Emily Dickinson has noted:

"Hope is the thing with feathers
That perches in the soul,
And sings the tune without the words,
And never stops at all"

Final Conclusions

If this author was not successful in writing a perfect book on the complex and vexed Osu palaver others "wiser" more informed and knowledgeable on the issue should continue the campaign for the eradication of the Osu caste discrimination in Igboland. Whether you agree or not with the analysis and conclusion, *The Osu Caste Discrimination in Igboland: Impact on Igbo Culture and Civilization* is a starting point for discussion and debate on the vexing issue. And everyone should get involved! As John F. Kennedy notes, "One man can make a difference, but every man should try." Let's join hands and abolish the Osu caste discrimination in Igboland!

Chapter 10
Notes and References

1. Wilbert E. Moore: Order and Change: Essays in Comparative Sociology. New York: John Wiley and Sons, 1967, p.3.

2. Henry Pratt Fairchild: Dictionary of Sociology. Ames Iowa, Littlefield, Adams & Co., 1955

3. Niccolo Machiavelli: The Prince (Thrift edition, Dover, 1992).

4. A. McLean and J. Marshall: "Cultures at Work;" Local Government Training Board, 1988

5. Daily Champion: "Abolition of Osu caste system commended" (December 29, 2005); also see Africans in America, Inc.: "Nnobi: Profile Of An African Slavery Source." The community in the early 1970s under the leadership of the traditional ruler *Igwe Edmund Ezeokoli II* abolished the Osu caste system in Nnobi (accessed July 22, 2005).

6. Daily Champion*:* Community Scraps Osu, Ume Caste;" April 8, 1989

7. Abraham Kaplan: "Equality"—In Hatred, Bigotry, and Prejudice (Robert M. Baird & Stuart E. Rosenbaum (eds.). N.Y: Prometheus Books, 1999

8. Okenwa R. Nwosu: "Osu Caste System: A Cultural Albatross for the Igbo Society;" www.nigeriaworld.com; June 16, 1999

9. Wole Soyinka: The Man Died. Harmonds-Worth, Middlesex, England: Penguin Books, 1972

Think it Through: Making Connections

"We have committed the Golden Rule to memory; let us now commit it to life."
Edwin Markham

1. What is prejudice? What social psychological factors contribute to prejudice? How does it relate to discrimination? What is discrimination (as related to the Osu issue)?

2. Who is an "Osu"? Why was the "Osu" made to live near the Market Square in the early time? What are the implications of the system? In your opinion, what are the geneses of the Osu caste system in Igboland?

3. Have religion, social development, and education effected your perception about the Osu caste system? Why and why not?

4. What are the stereotypes associated with the so-called Osu in your community? Do you agree or disagree with them?

5. Why is the system politically unpalatable in Igboland? What are the impacts on Igbo culture and civilization? Agree or disagree: the Igbo culture and tradition encourages the Osu caste system.

6. In your opinion, has the government (federal, state, and local) made any serious efforts (if at all) to resolve the Osu system in Igboland? What do you think were the reasons for the failure of the 1956 law against the system in then Eastern Region?

7. How is the Osu being treated in your community? Is there any improvement in the social interaction between the "Osu" and "Diala" in your community? If yes, what are the factors?

8. Could legislation enable the "Osu" to gain social acceptance? If possible, how would religion tackle the Osu problem?

9. Would you, as a "Diala" hire an "Osu" as a maid? Why and why not?

10. Prepare ten points that would give an outsider insight about the Osu caste system. Explain why each point is important.

11. Explain the social implications of the Osu system? Name some of the social problems facing the "Osu" in your community.

12. Would you, as a "Diala" accept blood donation from an "Osu" if you were sick (and it was your only chance of survival)?

13. What steps could be taken to dismantle the Osu caste practice? What are the dangers in using violence to affect social changes?

14. How would a society enforce any laws against the Osu system? Should the system be studied in schools? Why or why not?

15. What are Human Rights implications of the system? What is the Universal Declaration of Human Rights? What are your responsibilities towards your rights and that of others?

16. Would you, as a "Diala", allow your son or daughter to marry an "Osu"? What would you do if you discover that your loving spouse of many years was an "Osu"?

17. How is the Osu Caste Discrimination in Igboland a challenge for the Igbo culture and civilization?

Research Problems

"Great discoveries and improvements invariably involve the cooperation of many minds." Alexander Graham Bell

1. What are the problems facing the "Osu" in Igboland and how would they be tackled? Make a survey and write a report on the effect of the Osu caste discrimination on this group in your community.

2. Think of the men and women in your community who belong to this group. Ask each to answer these questions: How much has the system affected their social and political lives? What forms did it take? Has any progress been made to reduce the effects?

3. How many people and communities do you think are affected by the Osu caste system in Igboland?

4. Conduct an interview to find out what the older people in your community know about the origins of the Osu caste system.

5. Some communities have taken steps to resolve the Osu problem. What are the communities and what did they did? Are the solutions effective?

6. Present an argument for or against the inter-marriage of the "Osu" and the "Diala".

7. Compare and contrast the old Apartheid system in South Africa with the Osu caste discrimination in Igboland. How does the Osu system compare with any other forms of discrimination you may have experienced?

8. What rights are guaranteed and protected under the Nigerian constitution? Are these rights being properly protected?

9. Describe a time when you were a victim of discrimination. How did you feel and why? How did you resolve the problem?

10. What should the "Osu" do to resolve their social predicament? What do you believe are the reasons the Osu caste system persists in Igboland?

11. Discuss some social supports that could be helpful to the Osu cause. Describe any difficulties you may face in relating, as you ordinarily should, with the Osu in your community.

12. If you were to explain the system to a 5-10 year child, what would you say? What information is not yet known about the Osu caste system? How can such information be gained?

Evaluation

1. Would you recommend this book to your friends and for use in schools? Why/Why not?

2. What was the message the book was trying to pass to us?

3. How would you resolve the "Osu" problem?

4. Select the best part of this book. Why is your selection the best?

Index

978-0-595-45921-6
0-595-45921-8